soul stages

*Surviving and Thriving
in the Second Half of Life*

—

CHRISTOPHER
CHAMBERLIN
MOORE

—

Morehouse Publishing
NEW YORK

Unless otherwise noted, the Scripture quotations contained herein are from the New Revised Standard Version Bible, copyright © 1989 by the Division of Christian Education of the National Council of Churches of Christ in the U.S.A. Used by permission. All rights reserved.

Scripture quotations marked (NIV) are taken from the Holy Bible, New International Version®, NIV®. Copyright © 1973, 1978, 1984, 2011 by Biblica, Inc.™ Used by permission of Zondervan. All rights reserved worldwide. www.zondervan.com. The "NIV" and "New International Version" are trademarks registered in the United States Patent and Trademark Office by Biblica, Inc.™

Morehouse Publishing, 19 East 34th Street, New York, NY 10016
Morehouse Publishing is an imprint of Church Publishing Incorporated.

Cover design by Jennifer Kopec, 2Pug Design
Typeset by Denise Hoff

Library of Congress Cataloging-in-Publication Data

Names: Moore, Christopher Chamberlin, author.
Title: Soul stages : surviving and thriving in the second half of life /
  Christopher Chamberlin Moore.
Description: New York, NY : Morehouse Publishing, [2021] | Includes
  bibliographical references.
Identifiers: LCCN 2021024134 (print) | LCCN 2021024135 (ebook) | ISBN
  9781640654327 (paperback) | ISBN 9781640654334 (epub)
Subjects: LCSH: Middle-aged persons--Religious life. | Older
  persons--Religious life. | Aging--Religious aspects--Christianity.
Classification: LCC BV4579.5 .M66 2021 (print) | LCC BV4579.5 (ebook) |
  DDC 248.8/4--dc23
LC record available at https://lccn.loc.gov/2021024134
LC ebook record available at https://lccn.loc.gov/2021024135

♦

To Janice, who has supported me through all my soul stages and who helps make the second half of life well worth living, and to our children Alice and Douglas, who are embarked on their own life journey.

To my friend Gail Morgan, who has been an invaluable part of this project.

To the late Rev. John A. Sanford, who showed me that the personalities of the Bible could be understood psychologically as well as spiritually.

To my third grade Sunday school teacher at the Church of the Redeemer in Morristown, New Jersey, who instilled in me a lifelong love of the Bible.

To my colleagues and the members of the Brandywine Collaborative Ministries in Wilmington, Delaware, where this material was presented as a Lenten course.

♦

Contents

The Plaque on the Wall

What would it be like to live the second half of your life with real enthusiasm? What would it be like to live with purpose and direction, to be fully present at this stage, enjoying what life has to offer, neither dwelling in the past nor deferring your real life for some imaginary time in the future? What would it be like to live in such a way that you are fully open to whatever life brings?

Several years ago, a friend of mine visited an old country church in England. On the wall was a plaque dedicated to a former pastor who had ministered to the congregation during a time when another denomination was making inroads into the flock. From the point of view of the existing church members, these new believers showed entirely too much fervor for their religion. The members had a word to describe it: enthusiasm. From their point of view, it was a matter of pride that they should avoid this type of enthusiasm at all costs. Accordingly, the plaque on the wall read:

> "To our beloved former pastor, who led this church
> for forty-seven years, with no enthusiasm."

I have known people who lived the second half of their lives with no enthusiasm, or at least no enthusiasm I could detect. I have also known people who faced the second half with a sense of dread, seeing it as a step on the road to decline and irrelevance rather than an opportunity for new life experiences and for spiritual, emotional, and psychological growth.

The fact is that people of all ages today are struggling. News stories highlight the number of people succumbing to what some have called the "diseases of despair": alcoholism, substance abuse, and suicide. Even those who seem to have done well according to the standards of our society find themselves asking, "Is this all there is?"

I believe most people, whether they consider themselves successful in the eyes of the world or not, experience some degree of difficulty in transitioning from one life stage to the next. For many, the passage of years seems to threaten a loss of vigor, of physical attractiveness, of relevance. It threatens their image of themselves usually formed at a much younger age and reinforced by society. It is amazing to me how many words used to describe stages in the second half of life are negative in tone. We hear about the midlife person "in crisis" or the senior as a "geezer." Not only are these terms negative, they also provide no road map for negotiating each new stage, and they leave us blind to the treasures as well as the potential challenges of each new chapter.

The subject of this book is to look at adult life stages, especially those in the second half, and ask some basic questions: What's going on here? What are the challenges of this stage? What are the pitfalls? How is this stage preparing me for the next chapter of my life?

More than a generation ago, journalist Gail Sheehy gave us such catchy terms as "The Trying Twenties," "Catch-30," and "The Age 40 Crucible" to describe adult life stages in her bestselling book, *Passages*.[1] Many books by other authors followed that explored various aspects of the adult life journey. But while most discussed the psychological characteristics of each stage, few related spirituality to psychology or looked for the interconnections between the two.

There is a book that does just that. It shows a young person struggling to gain a sense of himself and of his life path as he enters adulthood. It shows men and women grappling with personal crises and changed perceptions of themselves at midlife. It shows older adults finding meaning and purpose in the senior years. That book is the Bible. It is probably the single most overlooked resource for people struggling to make sense of their lives and of the changes they experience during the passage from youth to senior adulthood.

The Bible offers no theory of adult life stages. It does give us portrayals of individuals at various ages struggling with the same issues people face today—issues not particular to any age or place or culture but universal to all human beings. These men and women portrayed in the Bible, these siblings under the skin, help give us insight into the challenges we face as we journey from young adulthood to the senior years.

In this book, I draw upon my own life experience and the life experiences of others I have known, as well as the remarkable personalities of scripture. I approach the Bible not only spiritually but *psychologically*. By that I mean I look at these individuals of the two testaments in terms of their psychological dynamics and how that speaks to the lived experience of people today.

The stories in the Hebrew Bible about the young Joseph stumbling his way into adulthood, the midlife Jacob struggling to reconcile two sides of his personality, or the older adult Nehemiah creating a legacy to pass on to the next generation are stories that could be about ourselves or our neighbor next door. These stories are universal. They shed light on our path as we negotiate our own confusing adult life journey.

The sequence I follow is roughly chronological. I begin with our experience of young adulthood and our active adult years, discuss midlife, and conclude with a focus on the second half of life and the senior years. Although the issues are presented chronologically, many are common to all stages; these issues accompany us throughout life. The good news is that each stage of life is a "soul stage"—a chance to start over, to get it right, or at least a little righter than we did the last time.

In this book, we will explore:

- What challenges did we experience as a young adult? How did we find our own path? What mistakes did we make? Did we avoid getting "stuck," and how did we get out of it if we were? Is failure always a terrible thing, or can it lead to greater rewards and life satisfaction?

- What did it mean for us to gain some measure of worldly success during what society calls the "prime of life"? Is "success" always a good thing or are there pitfalls? Did we give up something to follow the expectations of society? How do we discover what we gave up and how do we reclaim it for ourselves?

- What really happens at midlife? Did we experience a "crisis," or did we use midlife as an opportunity to change direction? Did the things that once satisfied us begin to seem hollow? How do we discover a new path for the second half of life and rediscover new aspects of ourselves? How does spirituality come into play, and how do we integrate it into our life?

- And finally, in the senior years, how do we reinvent ourselves? Where do we find energy and passion? Do we have a legacy to leave for the next generation, and how do we figure out what that might be? Are the senior years a time for retreating from life, or can they be something much more?

As I investigate these questions, I will use examples from my own life and from my pastoral experience gained over forty years as an ordained leader in the church. I will use the narratives of biblical personalities as reference points. Above all, I will ask you to bring your own life into the discussion. What have you experienced? Where have you failed? Where have you succeeded? What is the next chapter of your life? What will it look like when you are there? And how can you begin preparing for it right now?

The adventure is ready to begin. Let us explore what God has in store for us.

CHAPTER 1

What Are You Seeking?

I only wanted to try to live in accord with the promptings which came from my true self. Why was that so very difficult?

—Hermann Hesse, *Demian*

Think of yourself at seventeen. Who were you? Where did you live? What were your concerns, preoccupations? How did you spend your day? What were you *seeking*?

If you had to choose one item from when you were a teenager—a photo or a memento—that would suggest who you were at that time and what you wanted to be, what would that be?

I know what it would be for me.

It is a newspaper column pasted in a scrapbook with a brown cover on the bottom shelf of a bookcase in my study. When I was a junior in high school, I achieved a small personal milestone. I had a letter published in the *Saturday Evening Post*. The *Post* had run a cover showing a teenage boy at a school dance walking across the floor when he finds himself in a dilemma. There are two girls sitting, watching him expectantly. Which one should he choose? I wrote to the editor suggesting he should sit down between the girls and initiate a conversation. It probably wasn't the most brilliant suggestion in the world, but it was good enough to have my letter featured in the "Letters to the Editor," where it was read by six million people across the country.

I experienced a tiny burst of fame, at least in my own mind, and it was associated with writing. Shortly after it appeared, a friend of my mother who lived out-of-state phoned to say she had seen a letter by a Christopher Moore. Was that possibly me? I went down to the local pharmacy and saw a whole pile of *Saturday Evening Posts* stacked up on the newsstand, all with my letter in it. I thought to myself, "If I were in Seattle this week, or Portland, or Atlanta, there would be a similar stack of *Saturday Evening Posts,* all with my name in them." It absolutely blew my mind. And I'm sure it was a formative influence because later in my life I wrote and published four books and became a newspaper columnist as well as a priest in the Episcopal Church.

What was your formative experience? What is the iconic photo or keepsake from when you were a teenager or young adult? What does it say about you, about who you wanted to be, or who you wanted to become? What does it say about what you were *seeking* at that time in your life, and maybe even today?

A friend of mine had her formative experience at Yellowstone Park on New Year's Eve. She was in her late twenties and was working as a successful stockbroker in New York. She had come to feel, however, that her job was not what she was called to do. Something else was demanding expression in her life and it seemed to have something to do with serving God. Accordingly, she took a year off from work and went to Yellowstone to live and work while she sorted things out. That particular New Year's Eve, she made her way from the hotel through the snow to Old Faithful Geyser, a spot where thousands of tourists gather each summer. There, on New Year's

Eve, in the snow and the silence, she watched the geyser erupt. That evening she made the life-changing decision to leave her work as a stockbroker and enter the Christian ministry. Her decision was the result of questions she had been asking herself: What am I seeking? Where is God calling me to be? What am I meant to do with my life? What is my sacred dream? What is my mission?

Millenia before her, a teenager was asked these same questions. His name was Joseph, and his story is told in Genesis.

Joseph's Story and Our Story

Before we meet Joseph, we need to ask: What does a Hebrew teenager living in the ancient Near East have to teach us about our formative years growing up in the modern world?

Two things. First, the human psyche has not fundamentally changed in the thousands of years that modern humans have been on the planet. Culture has changed. Society has changed. The physical environment has changed. Technology has changed in unimaginable ways. But the actual human psyche—that mental and emotional hardwiring of what it means to be human—has not substantially changed, if at all, in thousands of years.

Put Joseph in a Phillies sweatshirt, give him a fashionable haircut, and teach him American English, and there is no reason why he could not pass for a twenty-first-century American teenager. His psychological dynamics as he came of age are not dissimilar from that of a kid coming of age in Cincinnati or Detroit or Los Angeles in twenty-first-century America. Despite social and cultural differences, psychologically Joseph is our sibling under the skin.

Second, Joseph's story is relevant because it is a product of what is called the oral tradition. Joseph's story, like all the stories in the Bible, was told word-of-mouth from one person to another before it was written down. An oral tradition has an important characteristic. The story becomes more effective every time it is told. Extraneous elements are eliminated. The parts of the story that resonate more strongly with the hearers are given greater emphasis. Over time, the story becomes a better and more truthful perception of human nature.

Joseph's story was told repeatedly over many centuries. Over time, the story evolved from that of a teen living in a particular time and place to become a story of all teens living in all times and all places. Joseph's story is *our* story of the difficult journey from late adolescence to young adulthood. It is a template for becoming an adult: the timeless human drama of venturing forth, facing trials, and coming of age—what Joseph Campbell called "the hero's journey."[2]

When we first meet Joseph in Genesis 37, he is seventeen. The Bible says this specifically, four lines into the story. The specificity about age is unusual for scripture. Even with Jesus, only one of the Gospels says that he was "about thirty years of age" when he began his ministry.

Second, he comes from what today would be considered a dysfunctional family. Joseph and his eleven brothers are the products of his elderly father and three different women. Joseph is the son of the beloved Rachel, his father's great love. His father's preference for him is obvious to his brothers and, as Genesis notes, "they hated him, and could not speak peaceably to him" (Genesis 37:4).

Finally, Joseph is a dreamer. He is one of those people who is in close contact with his unconscious. He also lives in a society in which dreams are taken seriously and often acted upon. Joseph, unwisely as it turns out, shares one of his dreams with his brothers. "There we were," he tells them, "binding sheaves in the field. Suddenly my sheaf rose and stood upright; and then your sheaves gathered around it and bowed down to my sheaf."

The brothers immediately recognize the implications of the dream. One can imagine the reaction of his brothers who already aren't that crazy about Joseph.

As if this weren't bad enough, he shares another dream. In this dream the sun, the moon, and the stars bow down before him. Talk about inflation. This dream is too much even for Joseph's indulgent father, who rebukes him and says, "What kind of dream is this . . . ? Shall we indeed come, I and your mother and your brothers, and bow to the ground before you?" (Genesis 37:10).

Joseph's self-absorption is getting out of control. He is "cruising for a bruising," as the mother of a friend of mine used to say, and the bruising is about to come. But first let's look closer at the nature of the sacred dream itself.

The Sacred Dream

Psychologist Aaron Kipnis distinguishes two kinds of dreams in the lives of most adults.[3] One is the practical dream that focuses on the demands of living out an ordinary life in the world, along with the rewards that come with living it out. The other is the sacred dream, which he describes as the "secret ideals of what we would really like to do with our lives," ideals that are often "irrational, unreasonable, illogical, impractical." The practical dream puts food on the table. The sacred dream gives fire to our life. The sacred dream and the practical dream are often in conflict. Providing for the day-to-day necessities of life keeps us tied to the practical dream, while our heart pulls us toward the sacred dream.

Probably most of us do not live out the full dimensions of our sacred dream, whatever that may be. Many of us find outlets for elements of their sacred dream in hobbies and part-time activities. The practical-minded accountant goes to the office by day and plays in a rock band by night. The marriage between the sacred dream and the practical dream is not necessarily easy. It drives many crazy. But for some fortunate few, living out their sacred dream becomes their life.

John Muir was one of those. This nineteenth-century American naturalist, sometimes called the "Thoreau of the West," was probably more responsible than anyone else for establishing America's great system of national parks.

Muir was always drawn to nature. Growing up on a rural farm in Wisconsin, he remembered how one night, as a boy, his father called him outside to see the Northern Lights. "Come, come . . . see the glory of God. All the sky is clad in a robe of red light. . . . Surely this is the clothing of the Lord himself,"[4] his father exclaimed to the impressionable young boy.

In his twenties, Muir, desiring a still deeper immersion in nature, walked from his home in Louisville, Kentucky, to the Gulf of Mexico—a thousand miles. A year later he moved to San Francisco, where a chance acquaintance asked him where he wanted to go.

"Anywhere that's wild," Muir replied. He went to the High Sierras where, in the summer of 1869, he experienced his sacred dream. He was assisting a friend with sheep herding on the eastern flank of the Sierras and recorded his impressions in a journal, *My First Summer in the Sierra*: "We are now in the mountains and they are in us . . . filling every pore and cell of us . . . thrilling (us) with the air and trees, streams and rocks, in the waves of the sun."[5]

John Muir had found his sacred dream. He became a mountaineer and an apostle of nature. In the years that followed, he went camping with President Theodore Roosevelt in Yosemite Valley and talked to him of the importance of the preservation of wild spaces. As a result, the national parks were greatly expanded under Roosevelt's leadership—and it all started with Muir's sacred dream in the Sierras.

I bet you had a sacred dream. Maybe part of you *did* want to be a rock musician, or wanted to start your own company, or write the great American novel, or be the next Steve Jobs. You may have settled for the practical dream, but I suspect elements of your sacred dream persist. If you are fortunate, you have even found ways to live out elements of it in your life. If you are extremely fortunate, you have found ways to align your abilities and your sense of call in such a way that you are living out your "sacred dream" and getting paid for it as well!

Joseph's sacred dream was his dream of the sheaves. Let's step back from the obvious ego grandstanding of the images of the sun and moon and stars bowing down before him and take a closer look at what the dream reveals about Joseph's ability and character. Essentially the dream is about leadership. Joseph's unconscious reveals that he has significant gifts for leadership, and that someday he would achieve preeminence over his brothers, as symbolized by the bowing sheaves.

It is important to note that the trouble with Joseph's dream is not that it's wrong; in fact, his dream is correct. Someday he *would* be in charge. A succession of people would recognize his abilities and put him in positions of leadership. The problem with Joseph's dream is that he does not have the emotional maturity to communicate it or execute it effectively, and for this we need to give him a break. He is only seventeen. The time will come when he will live out his dream and make it come true, not just for his own benefit but for that of many others.

It is at this point that Joseph's story takes an unexpected turn.

Joseph is summoned by his father, Jacob, and sent out to check up on Rueben and his other brothers who are grazing the sheep at Shechem. It is hard to know what to make of his father's request. Jacob must have known of the bad blood between Joseph and his brothers. Does he see this as a way of mending fences between his sons? Is this his way of forcing his boy to grow up and take on some adult responsibilities? Or is Jacob simply clueless, not realizing the depth of the estrangement and the danger he is placing on Joseph? There is more than a little of the absent father in Jacob.

In any event, Joseph sets off in his resplendent "coat of many colors" given by his adoring father and symbolizing, for the brothers, the father's favoritism.

The biblical account makes it sound as though the brothers are just off in the next valley, but Shechem, where his brothers were supposed to be, was as much as fifteen miles away over rough desert terrain, and Joseph gets lost. Being lost in the desert alone at night is a scary business. We can imagine Joseph going to sleep with the sound of the wind blowing against the mesas and the terrifying cry of the jackals off in the distance. Possibly the next day, as he wanders in the desert, he encounters a stranger.

Joseph and the Mysterious Stranger

The man that Joseph meets in the wilderness seems to come out of nowhere. The whole encounter has an air of the strange and uncanny, something one might experience in a dream. Given Joseph's propensity for dreams, I wonder if it was.

The stranger asks Joseph a very probing question, "What are you seeking?"

Let's stop and appreciate the strangeness of the situation. Joseph is all alone in the desert and suddenly a stranger appears and begins a conversation. If it is an actual person and not a dream, where does this man come from? Who is he?

Often, as we read the Bible, we tend to ignore or pass over incidents that seem odd or illogical and say to ourselves, "Well, I don't understand this, but it's the Bible, so it must make sense." Instead, we need to take notice of anything in scripture that seems strange or illogical because they are often the very things that turn out to be the most important. The Bible is full of strange encounters that turn out to be crucial in the lives of the participants.

Notice the question: "What are you seeking?" It should stop Joseph in his tracks. It is a question that should make Joseph say, "Let me think it over for a minute—or maybe five years, or maybe even for a whole lifetime—and figure out what it is I really am seeking."

Similar questions reappear throughout scripture. Later in Genesis, the angel asks Hagar, an enslaved servant of Abraham and Sarah, who flees into the desert, "Where have you come from and where are you going?" (16:8). The Lord asks the future king Solomon in a dream, "Ask what I should give you" (2 Chronicles 1:7). And Jesus asks his future disciples, James and John, "What are you looking for?" (John 1:38). If we were asked to name the most common question in the Bible, we might say, "Do you believe?" In fact, the most asked question probably is, "What are you seeking?"

I remember when I was asked that question, or rather I asked it of myself. I was teaching English at a boarding school in Connecticut. I realized that I didn't want to teach English grammar and composition to high school sophomores for the rest of my life. At twenty-seven, I was five years out of college and I didn't have a clue what I wanted to do. I decided it was time to get serious. I asked myself what, if anything, really excited me about teaching. I realized there were two situations where it really came alive for me. One was when my students and I were discussing a reading assignment in class and the discussion veered off into questions about the meaning of life. (I'm sure I had more than a little to do with this "veering.") The other was when a student came to me with a personal problem and I was able to engage in some one-on-one counseling.

I asked myself, "Where does someone get paid for helping people with their problems and talking about the meaning of life?"

Ministry sounded like the answer to me. What I was seeking was a place where I could help people with their problems and talk about the meaning of life. Later that year I applied to seminary and began the journey that turned into over forty years in Christian ministry. And it started with the question, "What are you seeking?"

When you were about Joseph's age, perhaps in your senior year in high school, someone may have asked you a similar question, although they may not have phrased it in exactly that way. Maybe it was your high school guidance counselor or teacher or best friend who asked you what you were going to do after your senior year. Maybe it was your parents who were always bugging you to "get real" and decide what you were going to do. Maybe it was that nagging little voice inside asking what you really wanted out of life. At that time in your life, with all the distractions of being a teenager and everybody talking *at* you, maybe, like Joseph, you didn't even hear the question. Or maybe you heard it but ignored it and grabbed at the first available thing.

The consequences of Joseph's lack of self-awareness are recounted in Genesis 37. Joseph is asked the question, but he doesn't hear it. He doesn't realize the implications of the question. Like most adolescents, Joseph is not thinking in terms of a five-year plan. He is lucky if he is thinking of a five-*minute* plan. He answers in terms of immediate objectives: "I am seeking my brothers. Tell me, please, where they are pastoring the flock."

The mysterious stranger, this angel of the Lord, realizing that Joseph does not hear the question, responds, "They have gone away, for I heard them say, 'Let us go to Dothan'" (Genesis 37:17).

So Joseph goes after his brothers.

The brothers see Joseph approaching in his signature coat. By this time, Rueben and company have had far more than enough of their mouthy little brother with the good threads, and so they hatch a plan. "Here comes this dreamer. Come now, let us kill him and throw him into one of the pits . . . and we shall see what will become of his dreams" (Genesis 37:19–20).

The brothers seize Joseph, throw him into one of the pits, and sit down to eat. As they reflect, they realize that fratricide is a little too much even for them. They want a less lethal plan, but one that still gets rid of him. They see an approaching caravan of Ishmaelite traders bound for Egypt.

"Let us sell him to the Ishmaelites" says one, "and not lay our hands on him, for he is our brother, our own flesh" (Genesis 37:27). So they pull the terrified Joseph out of the pit, offer him for sale to the caravan master, and Joseph is off to become a slave in Egypt.

A Vision Quest

When I first read the story of Joseph, it reminded me of something from another time and another place, thousands of years and thousands of miles removed from the ancient Near East: the Native American vision quest as practiced by Great Plains tribes such as the Lakota up until the coming of the White Man and even after.

Lame Deer, a traditional Native American medicine man, describes the vision quest he experienced when he was sixteen, the traditional age for the experience:

> I was all alone on the hilltop. I sat there in the vision pit, a hole dug into the hill. I watched old man Chest, the medicine man who had brought me there, disappear far down in the valley. I was all by myself, left on the hilltop for four days and nights without food or water. I was sixteen. I was scared. Four days and nights is a long, long time. When it was over, I would no longer be a boy, but a man. I would have had my vision. I would be given a man's name . . . .
>
> I didn't know how long I had been up there on that hill. I felt a hand on my shoulder. It was old man Chest, who had come for me. He told me that I had been in the vision pit for four days and four nights. He told me that the vision pit had changed me in a way that I would not be able to understand at the time. He told me that I was no longer a boy. I was a man now. I was Lame Deer.[6]

Like Joseph, Lame Deer has a formative experience in the wilderness. Like Joseph, he descends into a pit. Like Joseph, he emerges as a transformed person. I am not suggesting that the cultures of the ancient Hebrews and of the Native Americans of the Great Plains had any knowledge of each other. Neither am I suggesting that the ancient Hebrews had vision quest traditions like those of Native Americans. What I am suggesting is that people of many traditions have performed initiation ceremonies as their young came of age, and that modern societies have no equivalent—or at least no effective equivalent—and we are poorer for it.

What marked your initiation into adulthood? Was it when you got your driver's license? When you went off on your own and got your first apartment? When had your first "real" job or perhaps your first child? When did it happen for you? If you are like most people, you will struggle to identify when that moment occurred exactly. Whenever it was, it is unlikely that the event marked you with the same compelling sense of vocation and identity that young people of traditional societies experienced.

In fact, young people of traditional societies had a huge advantage over young adults in the modern world. They had ceremonies to help lead them into a knowledge of their natural abilities and sense of calling as they were about to enter adulthood. If you are like most people in our society, you probably struggled for years to figure out exactly who you were. In fact, you may be struggling even today.

After Joseph is dragged out of the pit, his story continues in Egypt. He will go down not once but three times: down into the pit, down into Egypt as a slave, and down into the pharaoh's dungeon after being falsely accused of an indiscretion with the wife of one of the pharaoh's officers.

But Joseph turns out to be one of those people who always lands on his feet. As the result of a fortunate set of circumstances, he is appointed the pharaoh's right-hand man and administrator of the kingdom. Joseph's suffering, rather than making him bitter, transforms him into a large-hearted man. The story of his eventual meeting up with his estranged brothers (Genesis 45) is one of the great reconciliation stories in all of literature. A famine strikes the land of Canaan where the brothers and Joseph's father are living. The brothers journey to Egypt because they have heard that grain is plentiful there and they appeal for help to the pharaoh's viceroy, who is Joseph, but they do not recognize their brother. Using a ruse, Joseph sends the brothers back to Canaan, and orders them to return with their father Jacob and youngest brother, whom he has not seen in years. When they are all assembled, Joseph reveals he is the long-lost brother they betrayed all those years ago. The brothers are appalled, expecting retribution. Joseph, however, forgives his brothers, and sums up his remarkable life journey when he says of his brothers' actions, "Even though you intended to do harm to me, God intended it for good" (Genesis 50:20).

May we be able to say the same someday as we reflect on our life journey.

You Owe It to Me

Before we leave Joseph, let's return to something we discussed earlier: Joseph's sacred dream. As you remember, his dream was that he would be a leader and others would bow down before him, but implied in this dream was that his leadership would benefit others.

There is a great scene in one of my favorite movies, *Good Will Hunting*, starring Matt Damon and Ben Affleck. Damon plays Will Hunting, a math genius from a troubled background working as a janitor at MIT. When we first see him, he is standing in the hallway, his janitor's mop and pail at hand, studying a theorem the math professor has posted on the board as a challenge to the students. Will knows the correct answer. He posts it on the board. The professor discovers that the school janitor is a math prodigy and takes him under his wing, to work with him and develop his natural abilities. Will resists. He feels loyalty to his working-class friends, and his abusive family background has made him feel undeserving of success. He sabotages every opportunity for advancement that the professor provides.

The climactic scene takes place outside Will's apartment early one morning. His best friend Chuckie, played by Affleck, comes to pick him up for work. A conversation ensues. Chuckie tells Will the happiest ten seconds of his day is when he comes by to pick up Will and hopes each time that his friend will not be there because he has gone to pursue his dream. He challenges Will, "You got something none of us have." Will says that he is tired of everyone telling him that he "owes it to himself" to advance himself and live out his gifts.

Chuckie replies, "You don't owe it to *yourself*. You owe it to *me*."

What Will's friend is saying is that every dream unlived betrays those who would have benefited from living out the dream. It is a profound insight. If Joseph had allowed his sacred dream to be beaten out of him, thousands of people would have died; Joseph's leadership abilities saved thousands from starvation in Egypt. Joseph's administrative gifts encouraged the pharaoh to stockpile grain for the coming famine, saving Joseph's family and thousands of others like them from starvation during the coming lean years.

A sacred dream is a gift not to be taken lightly. It may even become part of our legacy.

Life Lessons

What are the elements of Joseph's story that make it relevant for us?

When we were young, life asked us, "What are you seeking?" At that time, we were, perhaps, too young to hear the question and answered in short-term objectives. We may have made personal or career decisions that were not in our own best long-term interest. The result was we spent some early part of our adulthood trapped in situations that did not draw upon our real gifts and abilities.

Also, when we were young, we were self-absorbed, which kept us from hearing the question, but the question persisted. Fortunately, life offers us many opportunities to get it right.

Throughout life, we encounter people who "get their kicks stompin' on a dream." They may be members of our own family, even our parents. We learned the sacred dream is not to be shared lightly.

Life presents us with "desert" times, periods of reassessment. They may come as the result of a life crisis or simply as the result of a need to reflect more deeply and they are not tied to a life stage. Adolescence, midlife, and the senior years may all be desert times for reassessment.

Early in life, we received a "sacred dream," a golden vision of who we were and who we wanted to become. Gradually, the practical necessities of life may have blurred the dream and made it seem impractical and out-of-reach. However, the dream never completely died and may continue to haunt us. Even if we believe we followed our sacred dream and are now living it out, life may now be sending us in a different direction. Fortunately, life gives us many opportunities to revisit the dream and live it out more effectively, as we will see in the next chapters.

Reflect

1. What were you "seeking" as a young adult? What was your "sacred dream"? What was the idealized image of yourself that you wanted to become?

2. What was your descent into the pit? What form did it take? Did this experience defeat you or did it teach you life lessons?

3. How are you living out your dream today? What aspects of your life help you live out the dream?

CHAPTER 2

Are We "There" Yet?

God will establish your line forever, and your
throne as the days of heaven.

—Psalm 89:29 (paraphrase)

When we hear the phrase the "Prime of Life," what images does that evoke? Perhaps we think of a time when things are beginning to come together for us. We may have completed our education. We have worked in some lower level, entry-level jobs on the way to beginning a career. We have begun to figure out our personal life. Perhaps we have married and started a family. We have learned, through painful trial and error, what our strengths are as well as our weaknesses, and we have mastered how to leverage them in achieving what the world calls "success." We finally feel that we are a competent adult in the world, and we have perhaps even begun to accrue some of the fruits of our accomplishments. We have now entered what the world calls the prime of life. And likely, we have not done so without some struggle.

During my twenties, while I was still in school, I worked a series of part-time jobs. I was a stock boy in a warehouse. I was a retail assistant in a pharmacy. I was a waiter in a resort hotel. In these positions, I was spectacularly ill-suited. I was not just bad. I was *really* bad. The system of stocking shelves in the warehouse remained a mystery to me to the very end, which came sooner than I expected. In the pharmacy, I could never remember what aisle the toothpaste was in and where the cough drops were. And the highlight of my career as a waiter was when I tried to take away a plate from a guest in the hotel when he was still eating off it, after which the manager of the hotel called me aside and gently suggested that perhaps my skills could better be used in some place other than the hospitality industry.

This series of job failures, which all occurred in sequence, did a real number on my head. I was beginning to question whether I was even a competent person, whether I was even employable, whether I would ever be successful at anything. It was not until a decade later, in my late thirties, when I had been working in my professional field for a few years and had some successes under my belt, that I realized that these previous jobs, as different as they all seemed, had in common that they all required skills that I simply did not have. I remember the moment years later when I realized, "Hey, I'm actually competent. I can actually do a lot of things well." This realization was a huge milestone—and a huge relief. It was also the gateway to what became for me the prime of life.

Entering the Prime of Life

Entering the prime of life had for me, however, another aspect. It was a negative one and it was something many of us experience.

It was what I gave up.

In high school and college, I spent many enjoyable hours in my room doing art. I painted. I did pastel portraits. I went out into the countryside and photographed historic houses. My last year in seminary I even took a course of sculpture at the local museum and did a life-size portrait bust. When I was making art, time flew. I would look at the clock and the next time I looked at it, forty minutes had elapsed. But then, after I entered my active years of ministry, my art fell away. It wasn't that I gave it up. I found I no longer had the time. The paints sat in the closet. The hobby that had given me so much pleasure faded from my life; the artistic part of me began to wither.

If the prime of life can be for some a time of living fully into the world, of fulfilling our potential, of becoming a successful person in the eyes of the world, it can also be a time when parts of us are packed away and put in the closet.

In this chapter we will look at the story of David. Before we look in more detail at the story of David and how it relates to our own journey, we need to begin by asking what our society thinks the prime of life is. Who are we supposed to be and what are we supposed to do during the prime of life? What does it look like? What does it feel like? How do we know when we're there? And what do we give up on the way?

Our best resources for answers may be magazines and newspapers. I went to the newsstand and bought a large number of general market magazines and newspapers, including many I do not ordinarily read. I leafed through the magazines and newspapers lying around our house. I focused especially on advertisements portraying men and women who appeared to be in what our society considers the prime of life. As I looked at the images and advertisers' messages, I took note of how these people were portrayed. What qualities did the images convey?

The results were sobering.

A substantial number of ads were focused on acquiring *stuff*. A bank ad showed a couple in their multimillion-dollar house, an arched hallway in the background stretching into infinity and gilt-framed portraits on the walls. Another ad showed a forty-something couple with an air of casual elegance looking out the window of their Manhattan penthouse at the city far below.

The ads that weren't about stuff were generally about maintaining appearances: about "keeping your edge." An athletic-looking guy was jacking up his T-shirt and displaying an impressive six-pack while he declared, "Amazing abs start somewhere." A grim-looking guy on a weight bench doing curls stated his philosophy of life: "Push your limits. Then push further." One prime of life dad was pictured at the front door of his house, surrounded by kids, with camping equipment ready to be loaded up in the car. The statement "Dads don't take sick days" was superimposed over the photo. In the bottom half of the ad the same guy was zonked out in bed, courtesy of a sleep medication.

The messages are clear. Living in the prime of life is about stuff: the house, the possessions. It's about keeping your edge: pushing, and then pushing harder, maintaining those great abs. Finally, it's about never taking a day off: being constantly on call—for your family, your job, your life—and then collapsing from exhaustion.

No wonder people have heart attacks during their "prime" years.

Is this really the prime of life?

As revealing as what the pictures show is what they leave out. Where is any sense of spirituality? Where is leisure and time off? Where is any sense of community? Where is art or music or any kind of creative expression? Where is any focus on making the world a better place?

All those things are missing.

We know, on one level, that advertisements do not reflect real life, at least the life that most of us live. We look at the ads and say, "Well, they're selling a product. What they're representing does not reflect my life." We know this on an intellectual level. But on another level, a subliminal one, the ads seep into our consciousness. In a subtle way, they condition what we believe it is to be a successful person in the prime of life. On some level, we come to believe that it really *is* all about the great abs, the high-rise penthouse, pushing and then pushing harder. And we become diminished as a result.

What does it mean to be in the prime of life? What would that even look like? And what are some of the dangers?

The books of 1 and 2 Samuel in the Hebrew Bible tell the story of David. If ever there was a person who represented the hero for a particular culture, it was King David for ancient Israel. His story is an inspiring tale of the hero's journey. However, it is also a cautionary one about the pitfalls along the way.

David, the Hero

If you visit the Piazza della Signoria in Florence, Italy, you will see Michelangelo's gigantic statue of David. At almost eighteen feet, the size of a two-story building, the statue towers over the Piazza. The figure itself is two and a half times life-size. When the statue was completed, it took forty men four days to move it half a mile from Michelangelo's studio (where they had to remove the door) to its final location in the Piazza.

Its prominent location in the central square of Florence across from the town hall and the direction in which it was placed were not accidental. David is placed facing south, in the direction of Rome, Florence's great rival for power in fifteenth-century Italy. He stands cocked, ready for action, stone and slingshot in his hand. His steady gaze toward Rome clearly conveys, "Don't even think about it, Rome. Don't think about messing with our city." Thus, David has the perhaps unique distinction of being "the man" for two different cultures separated in time by two and a half millennia—Israel in the tenth century before Christ, and Renaissance Italy in the fifteenth century. The statue in the Piazza today is a replica of the original, which is now in the Duomo in Florence, but it is no less a fitting memorial for Israel's great warrior king.

David was the hero for ancient Israel in the tenth century BCE. His renown was reflected in his own day by what people said about him in comparison to his rival, the previous king Saul, "Saul has killed his thousands, and David his ten thousands" (1 Samuel 18:7)—the ultimate accolade in ancient Israel's warrior culture. For centuries to come, David was Israel's model of the ideal king, the one successive kings tried to emulate. The Gospel of Matthew traces Christ's genealogy through David. Even in our own day, best-selling books are written about David.[7]

We first meet David in 1 Samuel 16.[8] The prophet Samuel, who functions as the conscience of the nation, realizes that Saul is failing as king; God offers a successor among the sons of Jesse the Bethlehemite. Samuel journeys to Bethlehem to inspect these sons and perceive which one is the Lord's anointed. Samuel makes the seven sons of Jesse stand in front of him so that he can see, by divine intuition, who the anointed one is. Eliab, the oldest, is the first to appear. He is the tallest one and the most impressive physically, but he is not the anointed one. Samuel had made that mistake before with Saul.

After seeing all the sons in the room, Samuel turns to Jesse and asks, "Are all your sons here?"

Jesse replies, "There remains yet the youngest, but he is keeping the sheep" (1 Samuel 16:11).

Clearly the pickings are getting slim. We are down to the shepherd boy and, as the youngest, apparently was not even considered important enough to be summoned. Samuel tells Jesse to send for David. When David appears, God says to Samuel, "Rise and anoint him; for this is the one" (1 Samuel 16:12).

This part of David's story is a youthful fantasy that resonates with many. We want to be picked out of the crowd, to have our worth recognized by our peers in some spectacular way, to be unexpectedly heroic. It is the stuff of myth. If you are familiar with fairy tales and world mythology, you will recognize that we are in familiar territory in David's story. The first stage of what mythologist Joseph Campbell calls the hero's journey[9] is the path from obscurity to greatness. It is the story of the overlooked youngest son in Grimm's fairy tales, of the baby Moses in the bulrushes who grows up to become the liberator of the Hebrew people. It is the story of the young King Arthur who pulls the sword out of the stone to prove his worth to become king, Luke Skywalker in *Star Wars*, and, most notably, of Jesus Christ who was born in the obscurity of a stable. We may even think of real-life heroes of our own day, such as Malala Yousafzai, fighting for women's and girls' education in Pakistan, or Greta Thunberg, the teenage climate activist from Sweden.

When we read David's story of coming of age from obscurity to greatness, we recognize not only the beginning of the classic hero's journey, but also some of our own aspirations when we were young, as well as a time when we perhaps felt "anointed."

But if this is an anointing, it is a very strange anointing.

For one thing, no one in the household seems to know of it or realize its implications. His brother Eliab doesn't treat David any differently afterward, nor does any other member of the household. We wonder if David even realized what happened. What did he think of this strange visit of Samuel to Bethlehem and of Samuel's statement about him, "This is the one"? What are we to make of all this?

Several years ago, I was at a diocesan clergy gathering. I gave a brief talk and afterward we joined for worship. At a quiet moment of the service, the denominational leader who was a well-known and respected figure in the Church, pulled me toward him and whispered, "You have it." No one else heard him. It was a moment just between him and me. I remember feeling a little dazed afterward and asking myself, "What just happened?" I felt that I had received, if not an anointing, at least an affirmation both of who I was as a person and what I was doing as a pastor. I have remembered that moment ever since.

If we are fortunate, we may have received such an "anointing" at some time in our lives. It may have been something said by a teacher who recognized some special gift or ability in us long before we did.

It may have been the chance remark of some friend or acquaintance that affirmed us in some powerful way. It may have been when we received that degree, or that promotion, that we earned despite tremendous obstacles. This "anointing" may not even have been noticed by anyone else, but it was noticed by us. And that is what matters.

Battling Giants

We come now to the story for which David is best known, the battle of David and Goliath (1 Samuel 17). Israel is at war with the neighboring Philistines. David's brothers are fighting in the war. David's father sends him to take provisions to his brothers. David arrives at the battlefield to find the two armies encamped across from each other in a stalemate, which has now gone on for forty days. Twice a day, every morning and every evening, the Philistine's champion, Goliath, emerges from the Philistine encampment to challenge the Israelites. Day after day Goliath issues his challenge, and day after day there are no takers from the Hebrew side. As a loyal son of Israel, David is appalled. "Who is this uncircumcised Philistine that he should defy the armies of the living God?" he proclaims (1 Samuel 17:26, NIV). These provocative words are brought to Saul, the commander of the Hebrew army, and he sends for David. David repeats to the king his promise to go against Goliath. Saul urges caution. "You are but a boy." But David will have none of it. Accordingly, Saul fits David with his own armor, which proves far too large, and David goes forth to face Goliath, armed only with his slingshot and some stones.

When the Philistine champion sees this shepherd boy with a slingshot, he is filled with disdain. Who is this kid with the slingshot to go against the mighty champion? Is this the best that the Hebrew army can offer? Goliath and David exchange mutual trash talk. "Come to me, and I will give your flesh to the birds of the air and to the wild animals of the field," Goliath shouts. David replies,

"This very day...I will strike you down and cut off your head; and I will give the dead bodies of the Philistine army...to the birds of the air and to the wild animals of the earth" (1 Samuel 17:46).

Despite David's bravado, this Goliath is no ordinary soldier. The Bible says that his height was six cubits, which translates into ten feet tall. His armor weighed five thousand shekels, or one hundred and fifty pounds, and the head of his spear alone was six hundred shekels, or nineteen pounds. If Goliath were literally ten feet tall, not only would he be well over a foot taller than the tallest human being ever recorded, he would also be suffering from gigantism, an abnormality of the pituitary gland, which, if untreated, results in high blood pressure, headaches, nausea, and even physical weakness. It is unlikely that Goliath would have had the strength to fight anyone, much less the kid with the slingshot. Clearly the story as recounted reflects not literal reality but rather what David sees in his mind's eye when he faces Goliath. David perceives a formidable opponent that he has to overcome: formidable as a ten-foot man with hundred-and-fifty-pound armor. David brings out his slingshot and fells him with a single blow; the rest, as they say, is history. By confronting this crucial challenge and achieving his compelling victory, David is well on his way to becoming a hero in the eyes of the Hebrew people.

The story of David and Goliath says that to become the person we know we are capable of being, to realize our highest and best potential, we must sometimes break through the huge obstacles of fear and indecision. We must step out of our comfort zone and challenge ourselves to become more than we think we can be.

In my late thirties, I was a team member of a religious television program sponsored by the local interfaith council. The leaders of my denomination had gathered for a national meeting in town, and I had set up interviews with several of them. It was the last day of the conference and I had completed my interviews. I was watching as the keynote speaker, former Secretary of State Cyrus Vance, was being interviewed by NBC. I realized, as I watched, that I had not requested an interview with Cyrus Vance. It struck me as odd that I had not. Why had I requested interviews with several national church leaders but not with the keynote speaker of the conference?

Then the answer struck me: because I thought I was not good enough.

I was good enough to interview church leaders but not good enough to interview a former secretary of state. He was out of my league. I saw him as larger than life. My perception was unconscious. I was not aware that I had set the limit on myself. When I realized this, I thought, "Who says I'm not good enough?" Then I did one of the most daring things I've ever done. I went up to our denomination's communications head, who was standing nearby, and said, "Do you want me to interview him now or later?"

Without missing a beat he said, "Probably now would be best."

He spoke to Vance, motioned me over, and I got my interview with the former secretary of state. Looking back, I'm sure Anderson Cooper would have had nothing to worry about as far as my interviewing skills are concerned. Nevertheless, I took a risk. I felled my own giant. In that moment, I felt just a little bit like David.

Several years ago, I met a woman who took a risk and succeeded. Her name was Kitti Johnson, and she was reputedly the first woman to break into broadcast journalism in San Diego. Sitting in the studio of KYXY radio, she shared her story.

Her first job out of college was in a supermarket, where she announced the specials of the day. She remembers thinking, "What I want to do is somehow similar to this, but it is not this." Accordingly, she spoke to the station manager of the local radio station and convinced him to take her on as an announcer. It was a hard sell. At that point there were no women in broadcasting in San Diego. It was entirely a male field. Women's voices did not carry "authority," she was told. What she said on air would not be taken seriously. Finally, over reservations, the station manager took her on. Her challenges did not end with her hiring. On more than one occasion, she found her equipment had been sabotaged. She suspected her male colleagues, who resented her presence. Nevertheless, she persisted and, at the time I spoke to her, she had taken her place as one of the best-loved broadcasters in San Diego. She had slain her share of Goliaths and had prevailed.

Are We There Yet?

David was "anointed" in that secret ceremony in Bethlehem that appears to have changed no one, including even David himself. Following his triumph over Goliath, we read that his fame became very great and that he "reigned over all Israel" (2 Samuel 8:15). As David's story unfolds, we read that David and his household "settled in the towns of Hebron . . . and there they anointed David king over the house of Judah"—another "anointing" (2 Samuel 2:3–4). Still later, we read that "all the tribes of Israel came to David at Hebron, and said . . . 'It is you who shall be shepherd of my people Israel'" and they anointed David king over Israel (2 Samuel 5:1–2).

The first time I read this account, I thought, "Wait a minute. So, is he anointed or not? What's this with all these multiple anointings?" I had to go back through the text and do some research into Hebrew history to discover the explanation. The first anointing at Bethlehem was God's recognition through Samuel the prophet that David was destined to be king. The second anointing at Hebron made David king over Judah, the southern half of the kingdom of Israel. The final anointing, also at Hebron, made David king over all Israel. My initial confusion revealed important questions about the prime of life in our society: When exactly do we achieve it? When do we really become the person we are trying to be? To put it another way, "Are we there yet?"

I remember an old television commercial that showed a senior executive sitting at his desk in an enormous office. His assistant comes in and the two discuss some corporate strategy. The senior executive approves a plan and then says, "That way we can sock it to the man." The junior executive looks puzzled. He looks around this gigantic office and says, "But you *are* the man."

This is the dilemma: If our whole life has been focused on outward success and external validation, how do we know when we have achieved it? How do we know when we are "there"? And what exactly is the "there" that we have finally achieved? All of us have known individuals whose lives became endless pursuits of more and more and more. More promotions, more achievements, more money, more recognition. Achieving success in the prime of life, as our society defines it, can not only leave us dissatisfied, it can also lead to some tragic dead-ends, as we will see as we examine the last chapter of David's life.

When Success Isn't Enough

David triumphed more than he could possibly have imagined. From his origins as a simple shepherd boy, he became Israel's mighty warrior king. He vanquished all his enemies and achieved peace in his kingdom. Second Samuel 8:15 tells us that "David reigned over all Israel; and David administered justice and equity to all his people."

Then the story of David takes a dark turn. Cue the music in a minor chord. Maybe David is bored. Maybe things have become too easy. Maybe the success and renown that David has achieved is somehow not enough. In any case, chapters eleven and twelve of the second book of Samuel tell us what happened next:

> It happened, late one afternoon, when David rose from his couch and was walking about on the roof of the king's house, that he saw from the roof a woman bathing; the woman was very beautiful. David sent someone to inquire about the woman. It was

reported, 'This is Bathsheba daughter of Eliam, the wife of Uriah the Hittite.' So David sent messengers, to get her, and took her, and she came to him, and he lay with her (2 Samuel 11:2–4).

David's sexual aggression will turn out to have tragic consequences. Uriah the Hittite is one of David's generals and will soon be fighting in battle for David. David conspires to have Uriah killed in battle. Uriah delivers his own death warrant—a note from David to Joab, the commanding officer, to have Uriah placed in the front lines of the upcoming battle where it is almost certain that he will be killed. All goes according to plan. Uriah is killed in the battle and David takes Bathsheba to wife.

This is a shocking story, even according to the standards of David's time. He committed rape and adultery. He betrayed his own commander, a man loyal to him. He engineered the man's death to cover things up and forced Bathsheba into marriage. It is hard to imagine a more complete betrayal of another human being than what David has done to Bathsheba and Uriah.

The prophet Nathan, an advisor to David, learns what happened and seeks an audience with the king. Nathan tells David a parable about two men, one rich, one poor. The poor man has a little ewe lamb which means everything to him, and which is a kind of household pet. The rich man has company for dinner and, not willing to sacrifice one of his own lambs, instead seizes the poor man's beloved ewe lamb. David is incensed and exclaims, "The man who has done this deserves to die" (2 Samuel 12:5).

Nathan looks David in the eye and says, "You are the man!" (2 Samuel 12:7).

"You are the man" is not a validation of wealth and renown and achievement. It is the judgment of an unforgiveable betrayal. David recognizes his transgression: "I have sinned against the Lord." The consequences are grave. The child conceived by David and Bathsheba is born dead, which he interprets, according to the beliefs of the time, as a consequence of his sin. Nathan prophesizes that the sword shall not depart from David's house and that evil will be raised up against him. In the years to follow, David's beloved son, Absalom, rebels against his father. That rebellion eventually leads to Absalom's death, from which David perhaps never recovers. David pays dearly for being "the man" in ways that he could not have foreseen.

Sometimes in pursuing worldly success at the exclusion of all else, we lose a sense of who we are; we sacrifice our decency and our basic humanity in the pursuit of more and more success, more and more of the world's favor and wealth. *King, Warrior, Magician, Lover*, the title of Robert Moore and Douglas Gillette's book,[10] describe the archetypes of the adult man in ways that we can relate to David. David excelled as king, warrior, and lover. As wise man, he was clearly lacking, and this became his downfall. In the context of twenty-first-century America, it is probably fair to say that we reward people for their prowess as transformational leaders, or what the Bible calls king (CEO, entrepreneur, venture capitalist), warrior (military leader, professional sports hero), and lover ("making it" with others). As a person of wisdom? Probably not so much. And this is the area where many of us need to grow.

Life Lessons

What have we learned from David about the satisfactions as well as the potential dangers of living in the prime of life?

When we were young, if we were fortunate, we were "anointed." Perhaps someone in our lives recognized a gift or quality in us and gave voice to it. Or we may have recognized this gift or quality in ourselves. In either case, we felt ourselves called to a path in life. This sense of specialness may have faded. We may not even remember what it was. But it is still there, deep down inside, and ready to emerge, with a little encouragement.

We do not enter the prime of life all at once. There are multiple anointings, multiple milestones. However, if, during the journey, we lose a sense of our self and come to measure ourselves entirely by outward standards of success, we will continually wonder "if we are there yet" and never feel we have reached our destination.

Making your way in the world and entering fully into the prime of life involves overcoming hurdles and obstacles. Sometimes these obstacles are external. Sometimes they are of our own making. At first the obstacles, whatever they are, will always look like a ten-foot man in full body armor. Along the journey, we may encounter envy and jealousy. There will always be a King Saul trying to pin us to the wall with his spear.

Living into the prime of life carries rewards, but it also carries dangers. We may find that we are losing important parts of ourselves. This may be the sense of honor and ethics that we had at a younger age. Or it may be the parts of ourselves that are not "practical," but that give heart and soul to our lives. Fortunately, we will have opportunities to reclaim these buried parts of ourselves during the second half of life.

Reflect

1. When were you "anointed"? What were the circumstances? What were you anointed to be or to do?

2. What marked your entry into the "prime of life"? What did you understand the prime of life to be? How would you have described it at the time? How would you describe it now?

3. What part or parts of yourself did you sacrifice during your prime of life? How could you begin to reintegrate these parts into your life?

CHAPTER 3

Crisis or Opportunity

Where have you come from and where are you going?

—Genesis 16:8

I was sitting in the big armchair in our living room, my four-year-old-daughter on my lap. The lamp was shining directly on my face and my daughter was studying me with the intense scrutiny that four-year-olds can direct at something that catches their interest. When she said, "Daddy, you're old," I immediately jumped into the age-denial thing that snags many of us when confronted with evidence of our own aging.

"Well, Alice, I'm getting older."

Again, she subjected my face to that same merciless scrutiny and rendered her final judgment: "No Daddy, not old-*er. Old.*"

Midlife happens to all of us. And while midlife is not "old," except perhaps to a four-year-old, it is unmistakably older. And for some of us, that is disturbing.

We struggled through our twenties and thirties and perhaps our forties. We built for ourselves an "adult" life. We fashioned some intimate relationships. We have, perhaps, a few successes under our belt. We are finally enjoying some stability in our lives. Then the ground starts shifting beneath our feet. We find ourselves doubting some of the commitments we have made. We question some of our basic assumptions. We find that some of our satisfactions are no longer so satisfying. We feel ourselves being pulled in new directions: inklings and glimmerings of new paths.

Welcome to midlife.

In the first chapter of this book, we looked at our young adult years. We saw how life asked us, "What are you seeking? What does 'success' look like for you?" In midlife we begin to see that maybe we didn't really hear the questions and, therefore, some of our answers have not stood the test of time.

In the second chapter we looked at what we considered our "prime of life." We saw how we tried to measure ourselves against what society considers success: money, acquiring "stuff," achievement, and rewards. We saw also how there were parts of ourselves— important parts—that we buried to fit the mold of what we—and society— considered success.

In this chapter we look at midlife, that transitional period between approximately thirty-five and fifty-five. It is a watershed period that marks the transition between the first and the second half of life. Swiss psychiatrist Carl Jung was one of the first to see that the second half of life as fundamentally different from the first. In *Modern Man in Search of a Soul*, he wrote, "We cannot live the afternoon of life according to the program of life's morning. . . . For the aging person it is a duty and a necessity to give serious attention to [themselves.]"[11]

Jung saw that finding meaning and purpose was a major task of the second half of life. "Among all my patients in the second half of life—that is to say, over thirty-five—there has not been one whose problem in the last resort was not that of finding a religious out-look on life. . . . None of them has been really healed who did not regain his religious outlook."[12] Substitute the word "spiritual" for "religious" and the point is the same: the second half of life is about finding meaning and purpose. It is about being more than doing.

Castles on the Beach

Jung personally knew whereof he spoke. He had gone through his own crisis in his late thirties, although the term "midlife crisis" had not yet been invented. Jung, along with Freud, was one of the fathers of modern psychology and Jung was in fact, for a time, Freud's heir apparent. He had fashioned a brilliant early career as a practicing psychiatrist at the Burgholzli Psychiatric Hospital in Zurich, one of the leading mental health clinics in Switzerland; he was colleague of Freud in the emerging field of psychology and professor at the university in Zurich. His writings were attracting notice. He had married well—the second wealthiest heiress in Switzerland. He and his wife, Emma, a noted scholar in her own right, lived with their five children in a lakeside mansion outside Zurich.

Then, in his late thirties, his life changed. For some time he had been troubled by what he considered an overemphasis on sexuality in the theories of Freud. In addition, he had a personal reason for concern. In working with his patients at the Burgholzli Hospital, he had observed contents in their dreams and fantasies much like what he had observed in his own unconscious. Was he going mad? Jung would not have been the first mental health worker to wonder if his patients were driving him mad, but he probably could not help but wonder if he himself would someday be in Burgholzli—this time not as a practicing psychiatrist but as a patient.

Jung knew he could not continue on his present path. He needed to sort things out. He went ahead with the publication of an article that he knew would cause a final break with Freud. He resigned his position in the university. He put his writing on hold and gave himself over to intense inner reflection, paying close attention to what his dreams and fantasies were trying to reveal to him.

One strong image that came to mind was a memory of himself as a boy of ten building miniature stone castles, even a whole village, on the beach. He had felt most himself then and he realized that this ten-year-old boy was still alive in him. He realized that to gain the insights he was seeking, he needed to return to the mindset of that ten-year-old. Each day after lunch, before seeing patients later in the afternoon, he went to the lakeshore behind his house and built castles and a stone village.

Jung's return to the playful world of childhood bore fruit. Reentering the fantasy world of his boyhood helped unlock his unconscious. Dreams and fantasies followed, some highly disturbing, others intensely compelling. Out of it all a significance seemed to be revealing itself. His unconscious seemed to have a purpose, and the purpose appeared to be the revealing of hidden layers of his unconscious. While working with these images, Jung realized that the truths that were revealed to him had relevance not only for himself personally, but for all humanity. Out of this a new psychology and a whole new view of the human person began to emerge. Almost fifty years later, Jung wrote, "All my works, all my creative activity, has come from those initial fantasies and dreams. . . . Everything that I accomplished in later life was already contained in them."[13]

Over the next half century, Jung published his great works on individuation, typology, and the interface of religion and psychology. He created a psychology of inner meaning to stand beside Freud's psychology of repressed sexuality. He remained active as a therapist, a writer, and an exponent of "depth psychology" until his death almost half a century later.

And it all started with a midlife crisis and sand castles on the beach.

New Paths of Service

My own midlife journey was much less dramatic than Jung's, but perhaps more typical for most people. It occurred at fifty-seven. Obviously, that is late for "midlife." Chalk it up to my American tendency to deny aging and to the accident of my genes, for which I take absolutely no credit but which had enabled me to look and act ten to fifteen years younger than my chronological age. For about five years, I had been highly engaged serving on a variety of church committees in addition to my responsibilities as the pastor of a large suburban church and the father of two active teens. One day sitting in my office, I thought, "I don't want to do all this anymore." It was not from a lack of energy. It was a redirecting of my energies. They were beginning to flow in more personally creative directions. Did I want to maintain my commitment to my church and to my family? Absolutely. To maintain my commitment to the multitude of church committees? Not so much. Consequently, I phoned the head of our denomination and told him I would finish out my terms on the committees where I was already serving but that I would not accept any more committee assignments.

I simplified my life. And it felt good.

In the years to come, I returned to my writing in a more intentional way. And I also returned to my hobby of painting, which I had given up thirty years earlier.

For some people, midlife is a time to enter a new path of service, often using the same skills they have developed over the years but this time using them in a new way. One such person was Richard Vevers, a London advertising executive, profiled in a recent newspaper article.[14] He enjoyed his job in advertising and was good at it. Nevertheless, he began to feel that he was called to do something of more lasting significance with his life and with his communication skills. A longtime diver and ocean enthusiast, he was shocked to observe firsthand the phenomenon of coral bleaching: the whitening of corals around the world caused by a two degree rise in ocean temperatures because of climate change. He was aware of how ocean ecosystems relied on the health of the world's coral to maintain the well-being of the planet's oceans. Using special underwater cameras, Vevers developed "virtual dives" where people could vicariously experience an underwater dive and see for themselves how the world's coral was being affected. The result was a film entitled *Chasing Coral*, shown on Netflix in 2017 that alerted a mass audience to the dangers to human and ocean life posed by the death of the world's corals. Vevers's communications skills and his hobby of diving came together in a new midlife mission to help save the planet.

The Tide Changes—From Doing to Being

How do we know when we are at midlife? How do we know when the tide is changing, the wind is shifting? What are the indicators? Midlife may be marked by some triggering event in our forties or fifties—the loss of a job, a divorce or separation, children leaving home, the death of a parent—that sends us, often unwillingly, into new directions and precipitates major changes in our life. Or the feeling may be more internal: a growing disinterest and disillusion with who we are and what we have become. Even after significant achievements, we may find ourselves asking, "Is this all there is?" Whether spurred by internal or external changes or both, midlife marks a transition from a focus on outer achievement and goals to an increasing desire to find an inner sense of meaning and purpose. Writer David J. Powell summarizes these changes in his book *Playing Life's Second Half*:[15]

First Half of Life	Second Half of Life
Achievements, gains	Integration, losses
Doing	Being
Outward and upward progress	Inward peace
Either-or thinking	Both-and thinking
Right and wrong	Both-and thinking
Finding answers	Living with the questions
Self-centeredness	Sensitivity to others
Living out of your false self	Living with your true self
Knowledge, information	Wisdom
Success	Significance

A midlife crisis does not happen all at once. And it does not indicate that the values of the first half of life—accomplishment, achievement, upward progress—are unimportant. Most of us try to make our mark in the world during the first half and to establish a firm base for our life by the time we move into the second half. But it does mean that at midlife we feel the ground beginning to shift beneath our feet and we find that what worked for us during the first half may not work as well during the second. The Hebrew prophet Elijah, whose story begins in 1 Kings 17, illustrates the dynamics of midlife, then and now.

From Macho Man to Cave Dweller

Elijah lived in the sixth century BCE, when Israel was moving back and forth between paganism, represented by worship of the pagan god Ba'al and Israel's worship of Yahweh, revealed to Moses on Mount Sinai. Elijah was a key figure in that transition. Ahab, the king, was a worshipper of Yahweh. Jezebel, the queen, was a worshipper of Ba'al. Elijah was caught in the middle.

Elijah is a powerful man. When he is around, people get hurt. He arranges a contest between the prophets of Ba'al and himself as the prophet of God. Elijah triumphs in the name of the Lord. Four hundred of the prophets of Ba'al are slain. When Jezebel hears the news, she sends a message to Elijah: "So may the gods do to me, and more also, if I do not make your life like the life of one of them by this time tomorrow" (1 Kings 19:2). Elijah fears the wrath of Jezebel and flees into the wilderness.

Let's stop the story at this point and reflect. Elijah, like many hard-driving, outwardly successful men and women of our own day, has lived the first half of his life through a combination of vigor and brute force. Up to now that has worked for him. He has prevailed in situations such as the defeat of the prophets of Ba'al. Now that is no longer working. His life is in danger, real danger. Jezebel fully intends to do him in. But we can also take his death metaphorically. How many of us arrive at midlife saying, "If I stay in this situation one more day, I'm just going to die." And sometimes, tragically, that literally occurs. Midlife is a time of heart attacks and other serious health ailments sometimes partially caused by a sense of despair we feel about ourselves and our situation in life. Or perhaps we take no action and "die" inside because we lack the courage to address the situation that is eating us up inside.

Elijah flees to the wilderness. He hightails it away from Jerusalem into the Judaean desert toward the wilderness of Sinai, far away from the clutches of Jezebel. Elijah is one of many in the Bible for whom wilderness plays a crucial role.

When we modern Americans think of the wilderness, we think of a family fun vacation camping or perhaps visiting the national parks. That is not what wilderness represents in scripture. Wilderness in scripture is a place of self-reflection and confrontation. It is a scary place. According to ancient Arabian belief, it was a place where one might encounter *jinn*, or malevolent spirits. The wilderness in scripture is not a place where one would ordinarily choose to be. It is notable that while two of the Gospels describe Jesus as "led" into the wilderness at the time of his temptations, Mark, the oldest Gospel and closest in time to the lifetime of Jesus, describes Jesus as "driven" into the wilderness. I think Mark's description is probably the most accurate. The wilderness is not a place one would choose to be, unless "driven" by urgent necessity.

Elijah flees a day's journey into the wilderness and stops under a broom tree, where an angel ministers to him. We can imagine this as an oasis experience. The angel feeds him, even bakes him a little cake, and gives him water but then sends him on his way. The suggestion is, he is not supposed to stay at the oasis. He is not supposed to settle in. He has a destination to reach.

Midlife can provide experiences of finding an oasis in the wilderness. Friends can be supportive. Therapy can bring us needed insights. But an oasis can also be a temptation. We can stay longer than we should. Or we can get distracted by something that seems to present an easy relief. We remember the old joke about the man who runs out and buys the red sports car at midlife. At midlife we need not tarry at the oasis. We need to complete the journey and discover at midlife, as difficult as it may be, the insights we need to live the second half of our life.

So Elijah comes to "Horeb, the mount of God." The name Horeb is unfamiliar to most of us. The fact is, it is another name for Mount Sinai, where Moses receives the Ten Commandments and which the Jewish people consider the Holy Mount of God. So Elijah flees to his holy place to seek the answers he needs.

Finding One's Holy Place

I suspect all of us have a holy place. For me it is the Appalachian Trail, two hours away from my home in Pennsylvania. I go there three or four times a year to think and reflect. I take the trail up to Sunfish Pond, a glaciated lake two hours up the trail. Depending on the time of the year, I may see only one or two people on the trail up, and perhaps nobody at all at the lake itself four miles in. There are times when I have been one of only a few people within a hundred square miles. As my footsteps crunch along on the trail, I become super aware of myself and my surroundings. I hear deer and squirrels moving about in the woods. One time a mother bear and her cubs crossed the trail ahead of me. As the hours pass, I have the impression of time slowing and the urgencies of my life dropping away. I remember one winter day when the lake was partially frozen, I spent the better part of an hour watching the ice as it slowly melted across the surface of the lake. I never fail to return from Sunfish Pond without a renewed sense of who I am and how God is working in my life.

At midlife, one needs to go to one's Holy Place.

Elijah comes to Horeb/Sinai, the mount of God, and lodges in a cave. I find the concept of the cave interesting. Some years ago, a book was published[16] that suggested that men feeling stress and pressure in life tend to self-isolate and go to their "cave" and hunker down. I suspect all of us tend to do that in times of pressure and stress. Caves can be very comforting.

But now Elijah's story takes a strange turn, as recounted in 1 Kings 19. Elijah is told to stand in front of his cave as God passes by:

> Now there was a great and strong wind, so strong that it was splitting mountains and breaking rocks in pieces before the Lord, but the Lord was not in the wind; and after the wind an earthquake, but the Lord was not in the earthquake; and after the earthquake a fire, but the Lord was not in the fire; and after the fire a sound of sheer silence. When Elijah heard it, he wrapped his face in his mantle and went out and stood at the entrance of the cave. (1 Kings 19:11–13)

What are we to make of all this?

Sometimes in life we want quick and easy answers. We are like the person in the old joke who says, "I want patience and I want it now." Unfortunately, life doesn't work that way. Sometimes we must wait patiently for the answers we are seeking. A friend of mine speaking about the first few months of her retirement said, "You try different things and most of them don't work out, but eventually one of them does." So it is for Elijah. He waits for the answer and eventually it does come, in the form of the voice of the Lord: "Then the Lord said to him, 'Go, return on your way to the wilderness of Damascus; when you arrive, you shall anoint Hazael as king over Aram. Also you shall anoint Jehu son of Nimshi as king over Israel; and you shall anoint Elisha son of Shaphat of Abel-meholah as prophet in your place'" (1 Kings 19:15–16).

Elijah finally has the clarity he is seeking. He is to pack up the cave, go back home, anoint two new kings, and appoint a new prophet in his place. (And we thought *we* had heavy responsibilities). But this clarity only comes—and this I believe is the point of the story—because he has been willing to wait. He has not rushed to judgment out of fear or panic. He has been willing to take the long journey of forty days and forty nights to his holy place, hole up in the cave, and endure the chaos and tumult of the earthquake, the wind, and the fire.

When you and I are in life-changing moments of transition, whether it was adolescence, or midlife, or perhaps even the early days of retirement, it seems like the chaos and confusion will never end. Our life will never settle down again. But if we don't panic, if we take the time to listen to a few wise souls, if we quiet ourselves sufficiently to hear what a friend of mine calls "the little voice that knows," which Christians call the Holy Spirit, we may see ourselves clear to new directions, in God's time. But it takes patience, and persistence.

Elijah's story seems to end abruptly with the anointing of his successor Elisha. We wonder what happened to this conflicted man. What did he do after he laid down his prophet's mantle? How did he spend the next chapter of his life? The next book in Israel's saga, 2 Kings, gives us the answer. We read that Elijah is part of a school of prophets in Gilgal, Bethel, and Jericho. I like to think that this difficult, arrogant loner finally found a sense of community and a new role as mentor, not only of Elisha but of others as well. Elijah discovers at midlife that he has a new role in life.

Finally Doing What You Really Want to Do

Midlife may be a time of changing careers, or at least changing the focus of our career. A wise person once said that at midlife we discover that we have climbed up the ladder only to find that it is leaning against the wrong wall. Several years ago, I wrote a book entitled *What I REALLY Want to Do . . . How to Discover the Right Job.*[17] It was a book to guide midlife career-changers into new professional paths. During the year the book was being edited, I worked with a supportive editor who was a former church pastor. At the end of the year, as my book was being readied for publication, he and I talked on the phone. He said, "I've really enjoyed working with you on this book and I just wanted to tell you that I've decided that I'm not doing what I really want to do in church publishing so I've resigned my position and I'm going back into the church pastorate again, and it's all because of you and your book." I wasn't sure how to respond. I felt like saying, "Thanks, I think." I hadn't intended my book to cost him his job. But seriously, I was delighted that my book had helped move him into new directions at midlife, and I wished him well in his new path.

Midlife can also be a time when we look back to the life we have lived up to that point, how it has shaped us, how it has made us who we are, and chart a new course for the second half of life.

"Gonna Take a Sentimental Journey..."

In the summer of my sophomore year in high school, my parents took me on a trip to the small town outside Hartford, Connecticut, where my mother had grown up. I saw the house where she spent her childhood and early teen years and where her father and mother, recent emigres from Germany, had a chicken farm. I saw the hill behind the house where there had once been an amusement park, already abandoned at the time of her childhood, and where my mother and her siblings played on the abandoned merry-go-round and the other rides. I saw the path along the cemetery on the way to school, where a group of boys once kidded her for her skinny legs. I saw these scenes and memories through her eyes as we revisited these sites from her childhood forty years before.

I may have wondered at the time why she wanted to go back to her childhood after forty years. Now that I am her age—and more—I understand perfectly well. Midlife is a time of looking back, and also forward.

There is a character in the Bible who is also called to take a retrospective journey. Her name is Hagar, and her story unfolds in Genesis 16.

Hagar has a complicated history. She is the enslaved servant of Abraham and Sarah. God has promised Abraham and Sarah a child, but Abraham is old, and Sarah is barren and, as the story unfolds, it seems more and more unlikely that Sarah will ever bear the child of promise. Then Sarah presents an idea to Abraham. Why not have him father a child through their servant girl, Hagar? Hagar has no agency in the conversation because of her lack of status as both a woman and a slave. Abraham "harkens" to the idea (I love the King James translator's choice of words in this passage), and forces himself on Hagar who, in due time, bears a child. As a perhaps unforeseen result, Sarah becomes jealous of Hagar for being able to bear a child and Hagar begins to lean into the status her child provides her. Sarah issues an ultimatum to Hagar and she is sent packing.

Hagar, having nowhere to go, flees into the wilderness with her newborn child. Here, like Joseph before her, she encounters a mysterious figure, an angel, who asks her a provocative question: "Hagar, slave-girl of Sarah, where have you come from and where are you going?" (Genesis 16:8). Like Joseph, Hagar doesn't comprehend the full implications of the question, and simply responds that she is fleeing from her mistress, Sarah. Hagar doesn't know whether she is coming or going. Her situation is indeed dire: no home, no prospects, and alone in the desert with her newborn child.

The angel's response to Hagar will seem highly unsatisfactory to the modern reader. He tells her, "Return to your mistress, and submit to her" (Genesis 16:9). On one level, the angel's advice accurately reflects the position of women—and particularly enslaved women—in the society of the time. On another level, however, the angel's advice perhaps speaks to a deeper human reality and one that relates to our own situation at midlife. At midlife, we may find that we must confront some difficult issues in our past, to "submit" to the past so that we may move forward unencumbered into the next chapter. Midlife may be a time for seeking counseling, or at least engaging in some deep introspection. Having seen more clearly where we have come from, what people and situations have shaped the person we have become, we can begin to assess more clearly where we are going at midlife and beyond.

We have now traced the first half of life's journey as it is reflected in the lives of three different biblical personalities. We have journeyed from the wilderness, with the young adult Joseph, to the palace, with prime-of-life David, and now, at midlife, back again into the wilderness with Elijah. We have also journeyed from the "sacred dream," with Joseph, to the pursuit of the practical dream, with David. As we now explore the second half of life in more detail in the chapters ahead, we will begin the long journey back again toward the sacred dream as we move into our more mature years.

But first, we will discover that midlife is a time for encountering new aspects of ourselves, as we will see in the next chapter.

Life Lessons

What have we learned from Elijah and Hagar about encountering midlife?

Midlife may be a time of dramatic changes in our lives. These changes may be precipitated by external forces—relationship issues, career changes, illness, empty nesting—that seem to cluster at midlife and that thrust us, often unwillingly, into new directions. Or the changes may be felt more internally. We may find ourselves feeling dissatisfied and restless, wondering, "Is this all there is?"

Midlife is a wilderness time. We need to leave the Jerusalem of the first half of our lives and journey out into the unknown. We may encounter a welcome oasis or two, but we need not get distracted or tarry. The purpose of the oasis is to give us the strength to move forward.

At midlife we need to go back to our sacred place. We need to rediscover those places and situations that have nourished us in the past. For some this may be nature or a return to a hobby, the workshop in the basement, or just quiet time alone. We need a "sabbatical" in our own personal "holy place," whatever form that takes for us.

Midlife is "cave" time. We need to hunker down and listen. It may feel as if the storm is howling all around us. The earthquake, the wind, and the fire may threaten to overwhelm us. We need to remain calm even in the eye of the storm.

Midlife is a time for patience. Wisdom, insight, and clarity cannot be rushed. They come in God's own time. Eventually we will be summoned from our cave to hear the "still, small voice" that has been inside us all the time. This newfound clarity, when it comes, will point the way to new directions for the second half of our lives.

Reflect

1. What was your experience at midlife? Was it marked by external changes in your life or was it more of an internal experience? Was it a difficult transition or was it more of a smooth journey from one stage of life to another?

2. How did you react? Did you resist, or did you welcome the changes in your life? What form did your "wilderness" take? Did you find a "cave" and what did you learn from it?

3. What new clarity and insights did you achieve at midlife? Have you been able to put them into action in your life? How is your life now different from the way it was before midlife?

CHAPTER 4

The Undiscovered Self

*"Two nations are in your womb,
and two peoples born of you
shall be divided."*

—Genesis 25:23

"Who am I *really*?" is a question that follows us all through life.

I go to my dentist's office and say to the receptionist, "Chris Moore for ten o'clock." Her jaw drops to the floor. "But . . . but . . . but *he's* Chris Moore." She points to a nice-looking young man sitting across the office who gives me a little wave.

I feel like I'm in the *Twilight Zone.*

The explanation, as it turns out, is pretty simple. My dentist has two Chris Moores as patients and, through a scheduling error, both of us were scheduled for the same ten o'clock appointment.

But still . . .

Who am I? Who am I really?

There is a party game where someone asks you repeatedly, "Who are you?" It goes something like this:

"Who are you?"

"I am Sarah."

"Who are you?"

"I am a woman."

"Who are you?"

"I am an American."

"Who are you?"

"I am a millennial in my midthirties."

"Who are you?"

"I am a medical professional starting a new medical practice."

By about the fifth or sixth response, the answers begin to get more revealing.

"Who are you?"

"I am someone who wonders sometimes if she really makes any difference in the lives of those around her."

By the ninth or tenth response, sometimes people are in tears, because they are revealing things that are close to the heart.

Who am I *really*?

The Santee Dump

Early in our marriage my wife and I moved to Southern California, where we rented a house and I settled in as assistant priest in a local church. Soon after we arrived, I became aware of a huge pile of junk metal dumped in the canyon between our property and the house next door. I asked my neighbor about the metal and he said that our neighborhood had been an orange grove before the property was developed, and the metal was the remains of smudge pots used to keep the oranges from freezing on cold nights. After my wife and I had been there a couple of months, I decided to do something about the junk metal. I borrowed a pickup truck from a church member and, one Saturday morning, I filled it with junk metal and took it to the Santee dump. That first Saturday morning became a weekend routine and getting rid of the junk metal became a personal mission. I would borrow the truck on Saturday, get into my work boots and jeans, toss a load of junk metal into the back of Mike's rattletrap Ford Bronco with the beat-up rear left fender and the missing tail light, crank up country music station KSON FM, and head for the Santee dump.

In the course of several weeks, I discovered that I really loved doing it. I looked forward to each Saturday morning. I was discovering another part of me—the country music, work jeans, pickup truck part of me—that had no expression during my work-a-day life as a local pastor. Anybody from my church who saw me in my work boots and jeans and baseball cap would have thought it was so *not* me, so not the "Father Chris" that they saw on Sunday mornings. But it *was* me, as much a part of me as what I did during the rest of the week. Would I have wanted to transport junk metal to the Santee dump forty hours a week, every week? Not so much. But as an adjunct to my ordinary life, as a complement to what I did most days, it was exactly what I needed. It was another part of myself. It was *me*, in a different guise. And I was even a little disappointed when I transported that last load of junk metal and my Saturday morning trips to the Santee dump came to an end.

The experience again poses the question, "Who am I really?"

If we think deeply, we realize that inside ourselves are multiple personalities that we have never lived out, but that exist within us, nevertheless. In Hermann Hesse's novel *Steppenwolf*, a disillusioned middle-aged man named Harry Haller enters a "magic theater" where he sees visions of himself in various potential incarnations.

> I saw myself for a brief instant as my usual self, except that I looked unusually good-humored, bright and laughing. But I had barely had time to recognize myself before the reflection fell to pieces. A second, a third, a tenth, a twentieth figure sprang from it till

the whole gigantic mirror was full of nothing but Harrys or bits of him, each of which I saw only for the instant of recognition. Some of these multitudinous Harrys were as old as I, some older, some very old. Others were young. There were youths, boys, schoolboys, scamps, children. Fifty-year-olds and twenty-year-olds played leapfrog. Thirty-year-olds and five-year-olds, solemn and merry, worthy and comic, well-dressed and unpresentable . . . all were I and all were seen in a flash, recognized and gone.[18]

Who am I really?

There is a story in scripture that explores the issue of different selves within the same person and how, at midlife, we often come to discover and even embrace new aspects of ourselves. It is the story of twin boys, Jacob and Esau, in the book of Genesis. Viewed psychologically, the story is an account of coming to terms with our opposite and reconciling the multiple selves that live inside each of us.

A Stolen Birthright

The story begins in Genesis 25. Rebecca and Isaac are expecting a child. Rebecca's pregnancy has been long delayed. Rebecca was childless and thought to be barren. This is a common theme in scripture and signals that a child of great significance is about to be born. Finally, Rebecca does in fact conceive and not only that: she conceives twins. The pregnancy, however, is not an easy one. The children are "struggling" in her womb. Rebecca complains to the Lord and receives some disconcerting news:

> Two nations are in your womb,
> and two peoples born of you,
> shall be divided;

the one shall be stronger than the other,
the elder shall serve the younger." (Genesis 25:23)

I'm sure Rebecca wonders what to make of this. It sounds like a riddle. But there is also something ominous in the sound of it.

Eventually she gives birth to two boys. The firstborn comes forth reddish in color and his body covered with a thick mantle of hair. These are characteristics of a newborn condition called fetal lanugo. The redness is the result of a placental transfusion from one twin to the other.[19] The second-born is normal in appearance but emerges from the womb grasping his brother's heel. This grasping quality will be significant in the story, as we will see. Rebecca and Isaac name their children Esau, meaning red, and Jacob, variously translated as "grasper" or "usurper."

The story jumps ahead to the boys' teenage years. Jacob has positioned himself in the family as a homebody, a man of the tents. He has a special bond with his mother, Rebecca. Esau is a hunter and outdoors man, a man of the fields who has a special bond with his father, Isaac. One can surmise that the two boys are not close, as is so often the case with brothers, even twins, if they are so different in personality and interests.

The crucial scene and the incident that changes both of their lives for the next twenty years happens one day when Jacob stays home, as is his custom. He is cooking a pot of stew. Esau goes out into the fields to hunt, as is his custom, but returns empty-handed. Esau enters the tent, smells Jacob's stew, and demands some for himself. Jacob, never one to pass up a chance for advancement and always on the outlook for an opportunity, demands Esau's birthright in return. In ancient Hebrew culture the birthright was a special blessing given to the eldest son by the father; it could also be transferred to another. Esau, as the eldest son, was the rightful recipient of the blessing. Faced with Jacob's demand for the birthright, Esau says words to the effect of, "I'm starving to death and you're talking about a birthright? Give me some of that stew." Jacob makes him promise that he will give up his birthright. Esau promises, and the deal is done.

Here are two brothers who are polar opposites. One is smooth; one is hairy. One is a homebody; the other is an outdoorsman. One is mamma's boy; the other is papa's boy. One is shrewd and calculating; the other is impulsive and blind to the consequences of his actions. Parents of twins often learn that the two children, although twins, are nevertheless often surprisingly different from each other. But these differences between Jacob and Esau are so extreme that we suspect that something else is going on in the telling of this story. The storyteller has some "agenda."

There are three ways to interpret this story. On the simplest level, it is a story of two vastly different boys growing up in ancient Israel. On another level, one offered by biblical scholars, is that Jacob and Esau symbolize, through their descendants, two of the tribes of ancient Israel, and represent, through their conflicts, the conflicts between the two tribes. But there is also a third way to view this story, and it is the one I find most interesting. Viewing the story psychologically, Jacob and Esau represent two different sides of every human personality. One is the public side that we allow the world to see. The other is our hidden, repressed side which, although unacknowledged, often contains some of our finest characteristics.

Modern psychology has given us the language to understand different aspects of the human personality: the ego, the persona, and the shadow.

The ego is the executive function of our personality. It is our conscious acting, willing, and directing self. It is our internal CEO, if you will. The ego enables us to perform our job, pay our bills, and plan our vacation. The ego also gives us the internal motivation to perform all our necessary tasks in the world.

Related to our ego is our persona. Our persona is the public face of our personality. If the ego is our CEO, our persona is our

Advertising and Public Relations Department. The motto of the persona could be "works for me." The persona embraces the positive characteristics that we have learned, by trial and error, work effectively toward building the self-image we like to project. People like me best when I am smiling and agreeable? Works for me. My boss values me when I am energetic and efficient? Works for me. My friends appreciate me when I am empathetic and understanding? Works for me. My male friends respect me when I am macho and aggressive? Works for me. Thus over the years we construct for ourselves a public personality, or "persona," that seems to work effectively for us in the world.

The problem is that we are not all these things all the time. There are times when the "agreeable" person is not feeling agreeable at all. There are times when the "energetic" and "efficient" person wants to kick off their shoes and stretch out in the recliner. There are times when our bravado needs a little nurturing. These unacknowledged parts of the personality come to reside in what psychologist Carl Jung called the "shadow."

The shadow is the repository of those aspects of our personality that we do not publicly acknowledge, that do not fit the neat confines of our persona. Despite the name, the shadow is not necessarily evil or ominous. Jung famously said that the shadow is 90 percent pure gold. What he meant was that our shadow contains aspects of our personality which, although unacknowledged by us, are nevertheless valuable and important and that help contribute to a more fully rounded personality.

When we encounter threatening figures in our dreams, we are encountering our shadow. These figures are ominous because they live in the shadows of our unconscious, far away from the light of consciousness. They appear as threatening and angry because they have been repressed and denied recognition in our lives. But if we can embrace our shadow, if we can integrate this "other" into our lives, we have the possibility of becoming a more complete and whole personality, and achieving what Jung called "individuation."

It is a lifelong process.

The story of Jacob and Esau is more than the story of two brothers in conflict. It is more than the symbolic representation of two competing tribes in ancient Israel. It is a picture of each individual human soul, struggling to balance different aspects of his or her personality and trying to achieve some measure of wholeness. It is a story of individuation.

A Brother under the Skin

Viewed psychologically, we could say Esau is Jacob's shadow. Not only is Esau everything Jacob is not, he is also everything that Jacob looks down on. He is impulsive where Jacob is calculating, emotional where Jacob is rational, has no concern for consequences when Jacob is always thinking three steps ahead. Esau is also an outdoorsman and connected to nature, while Jacob is a man of the tents. We need to think of these differences between Jacob and Esau to understand the significance of Jacob's stealing of Esau's birthright.

We remember that Esau is the firstborn and that Jacob's name means "usurper" or "grasper." What Jacob steals is what is not rightfully his, that is, Esau's "birthright." When we were born, our instinctive self emerged first. It preceded our rational ego self. Over time, as we grew to maturity, our ego self took over. It usurped the place of our instinctive self. It stole our instinctive self's "birthright," that is, it's right to live openly and unencumbered in the world. Even though our instinctive self came first into the world, it gradually lost its prime of place. As a result, it went underground to become our shadow. This is the bargain all of us make. To function successfully in the world, we allow our ego to take over. Other qualities which do not serve the ego go underground to become our shadow. And all of this works fine, until it doesn't. At some point in life, these other qualities reassert themselves. Our shadow comes knocking at the door to claim its "birthright." This often happens at midlife.

When we left Jacob, he had badgered Esau into selling his birthright for a pot of stew. In Genesis 27, Jacob carries the con a step further. His father, Isaac, still must convey the blessing for it to be effective, and for this Jacob devises an elaborate ruse. He must appear to be Esau to his aged and infirm father, who is also blind. When Jacob is called in to his father's presence to receive the blessing intended for Esau, Jacob dons Esau's robe so that he will feel like Esau. He takes advantage of Esau's hairiness by covering his wrists with the skin of a goat. Despite all this, his father senses a deception. He asks Jacob, "Are you really my son Esau?" Twice Jacob replies that he is. Jacob's con works. Isaac gives to Jacob the irrevocable blessing intended for Esau. The blessing granted, Jacob leaves his father's presence and, shortly after, Esau comes in from the hunt. Isaac tells Esau what has happened, that Jacob appeared to him and received the blessing intended for him. It cannot now be rescinded. Both Isaac and Esau are devastated. Esau weeps and asks his father, "Have you but one blessing, my father?" Isaac replies with words which will prove to be prophetic:

> "By your sword you shall live,
> and you shall serve your brother;
> but when you break loose,
> you shall break his yoke from your neck." (Genesis 27:40)

Family Conflict

Jacob pulls off his con and things get a little dicey, as recounted in Genesis 28. Jacob's ever supportive mother Rachel, who aided and abetted Jacob in this whole scheme, overhears Esau threatening murder against his brother. Warned by Rachel, Jacob packs his belonging and lights out for the territory, which in this case is the encampment of his uncle Laban, Rachel's brother. Laban lives far enough away to be out of the reach of his vengeance-seeking brother. That first night in the wilderness, Jacob goes to sleep and sees a vision of angels ascending and descending on a ladder between heaven and earth and hears the voice of God promising protection on his journey. Jacob wakes up and exclaims, "How awesome is this place! This is none other than the house of God, and this is the gate of heaven" (Genesis 28:17). Jacob, however, has a totally transactional view of life and views every encounter in life as a deal which potentially can be turned to his advantage. Consequently, he makes a bargain with himself: "If God will be with me, and will keep me in this way that I go, and will give me bread to eat and clothing to wear, so that I come again to my father's house in peace, then the Lord shall be my God" (Genesis 28:20–21).

Jacob arrives in Paddan-aram, the home of Laban, and is warmly greeted by his uncle. Laban exclaims, "Surely you are my bone and my flesh." Just how true this is, Jacob has no idea, because Laban turns out to be every bit as much of a con artist as Jacob. Laban cheats Jacob in his selection of a wife. He cheats him in the allocation of the flocks and herds. Uncle Laban is a piece of work. Jacob, however, estranged from his own family and threatened by his brother, has run out of choices. He settles down, puts his acquisitive skills to work, and over the next twenty years, in the words of scripture, "grew exceedingly rich, and had large flocks, and male and female slaves, and camels and donkeys" (Genesis 30:43).

Laban's own sons, however, resent Jacob's success at their father's expense. Also, of course, this being the ancient Near East, the arid land can only support so many people and animals. Clearly it is time for Jacob and his household to move on.

Jacob, by now, is middle-aged. Twenty years have elapsed. If Jacob was in his late teens when he fled home and came to live with his uncle, he is now nearing forty. One of the characteristics of middle age is that the things that worked for you in the first half of life start not working in the second half. Jacob's scheming and conniving have enabled him to achieve great outward success in this first half of his life. Now, at midlife, they have become a liability. He is estranged from his family and must move on. The problem, of course, is where to go. It is time for Jacob to return to his family of origin, but to do this, he must deal with the brother he had cheated twenty years before.

Jacob collects his household, and they journey across the wilderness toward home. As they get within the vicinity of Esau, Jacob sends out a scouting party to see how he might be received. The news is not good: "The messengers returned to Jacob, saying, 'We came to your brother Esau, and he is coming to meet you, and four hundred men are with him'" (Genesis 32:6)

This is the very thing Jacob feared: that after twenty years his brother still carries a vendetta. Jacob, ever calculating even in the middle of danger, divides his company into two, so that if Esau attacks one, the other may have a chance to survive, and decides to spend what may be the last night of his life alone on the bank of the river Jabbok, which separates him from Esau.

Why does he make this decision to be alone? Perhaps he is thinking that if Esau attacks his people, he himself may survive. Or perhaps, more likely, he simply needs to be alone to wrestle with his demons on what may be the last night of his life. The qualities that have worked for him during the first half of his life—cunning, conniving, taking advantage of others—are no longer working. They are now threatening his very life. "Works for me" no longer works for Jacob. He finds himself on the bank of the river, literally at a watershed in his life. The night is coming. He is facing a "dark night of the soul." And he is alone to confront whatever awaits him.

A Midnight Assailant

One of the strangest incidents in the Bible occurs in Genesis 32. A "man" appears and wrestles with Jacob until the break of day. Who is he? Where does he come from? Furthermore, this man seems to have multiple identities. Genesis identifies him as a man. However, paintings of the incident, such as the famous one by Gauguin, are entitled "Jacob Wrestling with the Angel." And at the conclusion of the story, it is revealed that the assailant is none other than God. Who exactly is this assailant? Man? Angel? God? What is going on here? Who exactly is Jacob struggling with?

The answer is all three. The fact is, when we have a crisis in our life, we are struggling with other people, angels, and God. There may be a particular *person* in our life who precipitates the crisis, so our struggle may be with an actual person. Since angels are believed to be messengers from God, this person or others in our life may serve as God's messenger in bringing us needed insights into our life. And finally—and ultimately—it is God working through our personal struggles, though our "midlife crisis," if that is what we are experiencing, to create in us a new sense of who we are and who we are called to be. So man, angels, God—every life crisis configurates all three.

But there is still another "person" in the story. This episode reads very much like a dream. It occurs at night. It is dark. A threatening figure appears. One could argue that this episode was in fact a dream experienced by Jacob on the banks of the river that night and subsequently told to others. In this connection we remember that when a dark, threatening figure appears in our dreams, it is most likely what psychologists call our "shadow"—that is, the unlived, unreconciled part of our personality. Maybe what Jacob is wrestling with that night, in addition to a man, an angel, and God, is also his own shadow, which he has repressed during the first half of his life and which now at midlife is reappearing to reassert itself. In that case, the story of Jacob and Esau is a double shadow story—Esau representing Jacob's opposite in life, his real-life shadow, and now this dark antagonist, Jacob's inner shadow, experienced as in a dream.

This "man" appears and wrestles with Jacob until the break of day. It is a mighty struggle. It lasts all night, culminating finally when Jacob's thigh is thrown out of joint. Now persistence has always been one of Jacob's strongest characteristics. Early in life he was persistent in scheming against Esau and stealing his birthright. Later he was persistent in serving Laban in return for his beloved Rachel. Now, twenty years later, in this nocturnal struggle, Jacob's persistence holds him in good stead. He cries out to his assailant, "I will not let you go, unless you bless me" (Genesis 32:26). Jacob receives his blessing and, with it, the gift of a new name: "You shall no longer be called Jacob, but Israel, for you have striven with God and with humans, and have prevailed" (Genesis 32:28). So Jacob's old name of "supplanter" or "grasper," referring to his less savory characteristics, is now Israel, or "God rules." Jacob's name now has a positive meaning, and one that will later attach to the tribe and still later the nation, of which Jacob will be remembered as one of its patriarchs.

There is a lot going on in this story. Let's unpack it and see how it relates to us at midlife and, in fact, at any other major transitional period in our life.

First, let's look at Jacob's persistence and the blessing that comes to him as a result of his persistence. Our society admires persistence. We admire the wounded warrior who struggles through physical therapy to regain physical functioning. We admire men and women who "gut it out" to complete a marathon or an Iron Man competition. We admire our professional sports teams who come from behind to win the championship. All this is part of the American ethos: never to say die and to struggle through to victory. But when it comes to showing persistence in the face of mental or emotional discomfort, our society gives us little encouragement and, therefore, we tend to fade.

All of us experience mental or emotional pain at various times throughout our life. It may come as the result of the loss of a job, the death of a loved one, or the feeling of depression and emptiness that we may feel during a "midlife crisis." Our typical response is to ask, "How can I get out of this? How soon can I feel normal again?" Perhaps we have recourse to antidepressants, so we can "snap out of it." A better response is to ask why we are feeling the way we are, to ask the question posed by the psalmist so many centuries ago: "Why are you cast down, O my soul, And why are you disquieted within me?" (Psalm 42:5, 11; Psalm 43:5).

That is a very good question.

Depression and feelings of emptiness come for a reason. Like pain in the body, they come to tell us that something is wrong. In this respect, depression is a great gift, although we tend not to see it this way. Depression and feelings of emptiness are first steps in rebuilding our lives in a new direction. Antidepressants are of huge benefit in helping individuals get back on their feet emotionally to cope with life, especially in the short term, but masking our pain and discomfort will not help us to answer the question, "What is going on here? What is this emotional upset trying to teach me?" Simply putting a bandage on emotional turmoil may provide relief for a while but will not provide the long-term answers we need to live the next stage of our life.

"Not Out but Through"

A story is told about Carl Jung and a patient of his, who dreamt that he was in a barrel of foul-smelling sewage that threatened to engulf him. He looked up and there was his psychiatrist standing above him. He cried out, "Dr. Jung, help me." Jung looked down, placed his foot firmly on the man's shoulder, and said, "Not out but through," and pushed the man back into the sewage.

Sometimes in life the answer is "not out but through"—not trying to escape from a difficult emotional situation but dealing with it and trying to find its meaning. For this we need to exercise a different kind of persistence, not the persistence of gutting through some physical challenge, but the mental and emotional persistence of trying to find answers. It is the time for some deep soul searching, for speaking with wise friends, for renewing or discovering for the first time a spiritual direction, for seeking out a spiritual director or therapist. Doing this typically is much harder for men than for women, because men in our society are so conditioned not to ask for help. To gut it out on the physical level takes a hero. To gut it out on the mental and emotional level takes a superhero, especially in our society. But this is the path that leads to the blessing. Jacob persists in his struggle and, as a result, he receives the blessing of a new identity and a new name.

A Blessing and a New Name

Probably every society recognizes the importance of a name. We may remember the Johnny Cash song, "A Boy Named Sue," about a boy whose father gives him a feminine name thinking that would force the son to fight for himself when his father was not around. Scripture is full of individuals who receive new names when their circumstances change or when they have a sacred encounter with God. Abram becomes Abraham, Saul becomes Paul, and now Jacob becomes Israel. Similarly, there are times in the life of each of us when we receive a new name. That name may be the inevitable result of changing life circumstances or of our own choice. We go from being a "customer service manager" to "retired worker," from "active parent" to "empty nester." This new "name" may be welcome or not, depending upon our circumstances and how we feel about our new identity. Sometimes we get to choose our own name. Sometimes this happens at midlife, as the result of deep soul searching and perhaps even pastoral counseling or therapy. "Angry and resentful" may become "finally at peace"; "frustrated and thwarted" may become "going my own path." These new names reflect a change of identity and, like Jacob, we may need to struggle with God and humanity to achieve the blessing. At the end of the struggle, we, like Jacob, may come out limping, a reminder that the fight for a new identity is not without cost.

The dawn has broken. Jacob needs to face Esau. The Jacob who goes forth to meet his brother—his opposite, his "shadow"—is very different from the scheming youth who stole his brother's birthright and who made a crude contract with God in the desert. Twenty years have gone by. The memory of that first encounter with God has stayed in his mind and undoubtedly has changed him in ways of which he is not even aware. He has encountered an even greater con artist than himself in his uncle Laban, and he has observed firsthand how much damage such a person can cause in the lives of others. He has known the love of his beloved Rachel and has fathered children. He has struggled with God and humanity and has received the blessing of a new name and a new identity. But now he needs to face the brother he cheated out of his birthright twenty years ago.

Truly to See Your Face

Unknown to Jacob, the Esau he comes to meet is also a changed man. Esau has gone through his own process of spiritual and psychological transformation. He is no longer the youth of twenty years previously breathing threats and murder against Jacob. He is now a man of forgiveness and magnanimity. We do not know how this occurred. This chapter of his life is not described in scripture. But Jacob is soon to see the fruits of it.

The two men approach each other, Jacob expecting the worst. Instead something unexpected occurs. "Esau ran to meet him, and embraced him, and fell on his neck and kissed him" (Genesis 33:4). And now occurs one of the most remarkable passages in scripture. Jacob says to Esau, "Truly to see your face is like seeing the face of God" (Genesis 33:10).

Certainly, there is no small measure of self-interested relief in Jacob's utterance, but something more profound is also going on. In this emotional reunion, the two are now one. The opposites are reconciled. The shadow is embraced. The "other" is now accepted as part of oneself. And experiencing this "is like seeing the face of God."

Carl Jung coined a term for what occurs when two or more sides of our personality are reconciled: individuation. It is coming to terms with split-off parts of our personality. It is accepting our shadow. It is forgiving yourself and others for not being "perfect." It is living into a new "self" that reflects your own uniqueness, but which also recognizes and accepts all of who you are. Individuation is, in the profoundest meaning of the commonly used phrase, being "comfortable in your own skin."

Achieving individuation is a lifetime journey. Probably most of us never completely achieve it or only experience it fleetingly. But when we even come close to it, it is indeed "like seeing the face of God."

Life Lessons

What does the story of Jacob and Esau teach us about discovering new facets of our self at midlife?

As human beings, we have a multiplicity of personalities. In the first half of our life, we learn what works for us and build a public personality, or persona, around these qualities. Other parts of our personality are ignored or repressed and go underground to become our shadow.

At midlife, these repressed parts of our personality come knocking on the door seeking recognition and affirmation. We may feel a strong desire to explore new interests and involvements or to return to some old interest or passion. Or we may simply feel a sense of boredom or ennui with life as it is.

The integration of the old and the new is not without cost. We may be wounded in the struggle. The key is to persist and not to settle for easy answers or a temporary relief from the psychological and emotional pain. If we do persist in seeking understanding, we receive a blessing and a new "name." This new name is an affirmation of the new identity we have achieved because of the struggle.

At the end of the battle, we have integrated the old and the new. We are now operating out of a new "self." We have achieved what psychologists call integration. To experience this sense of wholeness in oneself is truly "like seeing the face of God."

Reflect

1. How would you have described yourself during the first half of your life? How would you have wanted others to describe you? What words come to mind to describe your "public personality" during this period?

2. What parts of yourself were not being expressed? What interests, involvements, or personal qualities had to go underground during the first half of your life?

3. What parts of yourself came knocking on the door at midlife? What were the circumstances when this happened and what were the indications that things in your life were changing?

4. As you look at your life in the present, would you say you have achieved the integration you desired or is it still a work in progress? If a work in progress, what parts of yourself are you still working to integrate? If you were to receive the blessing of a new name, what would you want your new "name" to be for the next chapter of your life?

Encountering the Sacred

"Remove the sandals from your feet, for the
place on which you are standing is holy ground."

—Exodus 3:5

What was your most profound religious or spiritual experience? When in the past did you feel you were standing on "holy ground"?

I asked this question to a group of people in a class I was teaching on the spiritual implications of various adult life stages. Their answers were revealing:

> "I was reading *Aesop's Fables* as a child. I noticed that everyone was looking for the key to life. Somehow that made sense to me even at that young age" (age 10).

> "I was in church on Easter Sunday. I had this feeling of 'presence' and of being embraced by God" (age 10).

> "I was out in nature. I was in a field and looking up to the stars above. I felt part of all I was observing" (age 15).

"I was hiking. I got lost and narrowly escaped death. I made a promise to God that if I survived, I would follow him" (age 17).

"I was on a women's retreat. The presentation was excellent. I felt God's presence in the words of the speaker" (age 21).

"I was in the service. I had been wounded and was recovering in a military hospital in Japan. I was feeling this tremendous void in my life. I knew I needed God" (age 23).

"I was hiking with my family. I remember the silence and the sunlight. I felt embraced by God's presence" (age 36).

"I was estranged from my father. Finally, after many years, we reconciled on the phone. He died the next day. I finally felt at peace with him and with our relationship, and felt God had a hand in the timing of the call" (age 40).

"I was in the midst of a midlife spiritual crisis. Like Jacob in the Bible, I wrestled with God in the night hours. I resolved the crisis by means of an all-night Bible reading" (age 47).

"I received a cancer diagnosis. The night of the diagnosis I woke up at four in the morning hearing in my mind the hymn, 'Trust and Obey'" (age 55).

"I had great difficulty dealing with my mother's death. After a long time I finally felt a great sense of peace about her death. It was God telling me that she was in God's hands" (age 60).

These responses show that profound spiritual experiences can take many forms and occur at most any age from childhood to adolescence to midlife and beyond. At midlife one may find oneself questioning the superficial commitments of the first half of life and looking for something deeper. Paul Hawker, a successful television producer, recounts the circumstances that led him to a solitary forty-day hike in the remote mountains of New Zealand:

> Like many middle-class white males, I've had a fortuitous life with all the trappings of what society would deem success, including a great family. We laugh, cry, banter, and bicker, and also celebrate, accept, and enjoy each other. I think it's called love. Yet despite all this there was something missing, not quite right, a restlessness, a yearning. Without warning I'd be overcome by despair. Seemingly from nowhere, wave after wave of melancholy would wash over me and then recede, leaving me feeling alone, hollow, and a fraud. A part of me was missing, but I had no idea what it was. . . .
>
> The emptiness of not knowing the truth about a higher power had finally become too much. The first half of my life was over, and I wasn't prepared to live the second half the same way—hedging my faith in "otherness" with worldly goods and achievement.
>
> I had little to lose. I was a lost soul, directionless and confused. The unanswered questions had become as critical as life itself. It was crunch time. Time to discover what was and what wasn't real, and to risk all in the process.[20]

Hawker ventured out into the wilderness of New Zealand with only a backpack and a map, and in the solitude of forty days and nights found a new direction for the second half of his life.

Hawker's experience reminds me of that of someone else—a Hebrew shepherd who lived twelve centuries before Christ and who also had a formative experience in the wilderness. His name is Moses, and his early life story, told in the first three chapters of Exodus, is rich in human drama and has much to tell us about the dynamics of a person coming to faith.

An Angry Young Man

Moses was born at a difficult time in Hebrew history. As we remember from the chapter on Joseph, the Hebrew people were invited by the pharaoh to settle in Egypt. Over the generations, they increase and prosper. However, a new pharaoh comes to power, one who ominously "did not know Joseph" (Exodus 1:8) and therefore did not know the agreement by which the Hebrew people came to live in Egypt in Joseph's time. This new pharaoh fears the Hebrews' growing numbers and power. Accordingly, he lays heavy tasks on them and makes their lives difficult. Finally, he even takes the draconian step of ordering all male children born to the Hebrews to be put to death. During this fraught period, a young Hebrew mother gives birth to a baby boy. When she can no longer hide him, she places him in a basket of reeds and sets it afloat on the Nile, hoping he will be rescued by someone. As it turns out, not only is he rescued, he is rescued by none other than pharaoh's daughter, who is bathing in the river. She takes him to live in the palace. He grows up as a prince of Egypt. The baby is Moses, the future savior of the Hebrew people. Young Moses comes of age, Hebrew by birth, but Egyptian by culture and training.

At this point, we might ask about the consequences of growing up in a mixed household: a household divided by race, ethnicity, religion, or class. Many people, then and now, have the experience of growing up in such a household. This experience may create anger, stress, and conflict, as the young person growing up seeks to reconcile divided loyalties. On the other hand, the experience may trigger something else—a search for identity, a search for a deeper sense of meaning and purpose. A young person from such a home is confronted at a young age with the question, "Who am I? Who are my people?" Attempting to answer this question may propel the young person into a search for self-identity and, with it, a sense of mission, as it does with Moses. And so, anger and a search for self-identity are both present in the life of the young Moses.

Who Are My People?

One day Moses takes a walk. The way the Bible puts it is, "he went out to his people." This phrase "his people" is fascinating. How does he know the Hebrews are "his people"? Has he been told this by the Pharaoh's daughter? Has she raised him with this awareness? Furthermore, does he himself consider the Hebrews "his" people? Whom does he identify with, his birth people or the people of the culture which has raised him? Arguably, "his people" are in fact the Egyptians, who have taken him into their household and given him a place at the table with the grandees of the kingdom. The young Moses had two nations and two cultures struggling within him. The conflict between the two is soon to play out in his life. As Moses walks out of the palace and onto the streets, he is taking what for him will be the first step on his spiritual journey—a search for his own identity and, by extension, for his purpose in life. It is the first step in a journey that will take him ultimately from the streets in Egypt to Sinai and his "holy ground."

As he walks out and about, he comes across a confrontation between an Egyptian and a Hebrew slave. The Egyptian is beating the Hebrew. Moses is angry. He is more than angry. He is furious to the point of rage. He intervenes and strikes the Egyptian with enough force to kill him. Moses is now a murderer. If there was ever any doubt in his mind about who "his people" were, that doubt is resolved. His rage has unmistakably revealed to him that his people are the Hebrews, his people by birth. Moses looks around and buries the body, hoping his deed will not become known.

The next day he is again out walking about, and he sees two Hebrews having a dispute. He intervenes, this time more gently than the day before. One of the Hebrews, however, turns to him and says, "Who made you a ruler and judge over us? Do you mean to kill me as you did the Egyptian?" Moses realizes his deed is known. He hears that Pharaoh is looking for him. He needs to make himself scarce. Moses does what his ancestor Jacob did and what the Hebrew prophet Elijah would later do: he lights out for a territory far away, which in his case is the land of Midian.

He comes to a village of the Midianites, distant cousins of the Hebrew people, and stops at the village well to drink. There he encounters some women trying to get water from the well for their flocks and being hassled by local shepherds. Moses, who by this time we realize must be a physically imposing and intimidating guy, confronts the shepherds and sends them scattering, allowing the women to water their flocks. His act of kindness and courage is reported to one of the men of the village, Jethro, identified as a priest of Midian, who takes Moses into his household and subsequently gives Moses his daughter in marriage. Moses and Zipporah settle down and have a young son, Gershom, meaning "Sojourner," and Jethro gives Moses a flock of sheep to tend. We read that Moses is "content" to dwell with Jethro and his new family. Moses now has a home, a family, and a trade. The life of this conflicted and angry young man has settled down. Moses has two cars in the garage, a house in the suburbs, and a flat screen TV in every room. Life is good.

And then one day he takes a walk. A long walk.

The Far Side of the Wilderness

The Bible says Moses goes with his sheep "to the far side of the wilderness" (Exodus 3:1, NIV). One translation calls the location "the back side of the desert," another "beyond the wilderness." This choice of words suggests that in his search for better pasture for his sheep, Moses has gone farther out than he has ever gone before. He is in uncharted territory. He is "out there." This is a good description of what happens to many of us at midlife. We begin to question our first half of life assumptions. We feel ourselves drawn into new directions. We have gone not only into the wilderness but even to "the far side of the wilderness." This experience is exciting. It is also scary. But people who feel this pull also don't have a choice. They are drawn inexorably in this new direction.

As we have seen previously, the wilderness in scripture is frequently a place of significance. Our ears should prick up whenever we read that someone is called to the wilderness or drawn to the wilderness. Wilderness in scripture is a place of self-confrontation and of encountering God. Jesus is led (the Gospel of Mark says "driven") into the wilderness in preparation for beginning his ministry. The young Joseph encounters a mysterious stranger who asks him, "What are you seeking?" Hagar sees an angel of the Lord who asks her, "Where have you come from and where are you going?" Wilderness in scripture is often the beginning of the spiritual journey that leads finally to God.

Moses goes to the far side of the wilderness, to a mountain, to pasture his sheep. In the scriptural account of this incident, the mountain is identified as Horeb, but we know it as Mount Sinai, the mountain of the Ten Commandments. Now I'm sure Moses gives himself a "practical" reason for taking his sheep to this location. Perhaps he convinces himself that the grazing is better on the higher elevations of the mountain, or there is more water for his sheep. But I wonder if these are the real reasons. Sinai was known as a holy mountain to the Midianites long before it became a holy mountain to the Hebrews. The trails leading up the mountain were in fact pilgrimage trails for the Midianites. So why would Moses choose to go to this mountain? What would draw him to this "holy" place? What did he think he was going to see or encounter?

Moses's journey to the mountain reminds me of a scene from the movie *Close Encounters of the Third Kind*.[21] This 1977 Steven Spielberg movie focuses on Roy Neary, an electrical lineman from Indiana who is fascinated by UFOs and increasingly visited by subliminal mental images of a mountain. This mountain has a very distinctive shape. It stands in open country and is shaped like a pinnacle. The vision keeps recurring, day and night. It becomes an obsession. One day, he grabs a wheelbarrow and a shovel, opens the window in the living room, tosses dirt through the window, and builds the mountain right in the middle of the room. His wife, Ronnie, thinks he has lost his mind. She moves out, taking their three children with her. One day he sees a newscast showing Devil's Tower, a real-life rock formation in Wyoming, where UFOs have been reported. It is the mountain of his dreams and visions. Neary sets out to travel to Wyoming, where he will have his "close encounter" with the aliens and with a whole different level of reality. Like Roy Neary in *Close Encounters*, I wonder if Moses feels a similar obsession about taking his sheep to Horeb, the "mountain of God."

Like many people at midlife, Moses may give himself a "practical" reason for doing what he is doing, but there is also another reason as well. It has to do with his soul. It is about being drawn by God.

In my first church I experienced something that I have not experienced since in my forty-five years of ministry. I had new people show up the Sunday *after* Easter. Now clergy are used to seeing new faces at Christmas and Easter. We call them C and E (Christmas and Easter) people. I'm not making light of them. I'm glad they're there and I always hope that they experience something on Christmas and Easter that will make them want to come back. But it is unusual to see new people the Sunday after a major holiday.

The new couple kept coming back Sunday after Sunday. Once they had established themselves and I had gotten to know them better, I asked them what had led them back to church, especially the Sunday after Easter. The husband told me an interesting story.

They had awakened on Easter Sunday with a strong desire to go back to church. The problem was, they felt like hypocrites going back to church on a major holiday after being absent for so long. So they made a pact, lying in bed that Easter morning. They would sit out Easter and then start regular attendance the Sunday after. And that is exactly what they did. When I was finally called to a new assignment and left that church, they were still active members.

For those who are regular attending members of a church, it may seem like no big deal to show up to go to church. However, for those who have not gone for a long time, or who have never gone, going to church may indeed seem like going to the far side of the wilderness. What will the people be like? Will they accept us? Will we know what to do? Will they talk to us at the coffee hour? Will our kids like it? In fact, whenever my wife and I are on vacation and go to a strange church in a strange town, we feel these same misgivings, and we've been "doing" church for more than forty years.

If simply going to church can seem like going to the far side of the wilderness, what about deciding at midlife to put a career of twenty years on hold and go to seminary to prepare for a deeply felt call to enter the ordained ministry? Talk about the far side of the wilderness. In my denomination, and in most of the mainline denominations, the average age for entering seminary is in the forties. These people have really made a commitment to go to the far side of the wilderness, as have also their spouse and kids who accompany them on this journey. So Moses's far side of the wilderness experience is probably typical for many people who feel the call of God, especially at midlife.

Moses leads his flock to Sinai and there occurs the incident by which Moses is best known, as recounted in Exodus 3. God speaks to him out of a burning bush. What's interesting about the famous story about Moses and the burning bush is just how short it is: less than two chapters. Yet, along with Jesus's parables of the good Samaritan and the prodigal son, it is probably one of the few parts of scripture that even nonreligious people are familiar with. The reason is simple: all three stories speak to us on multiple levels about what it means to be human and what it means to come to faith.

Let's unpack this story and see what it is saying to us.

When Moses encounters the burning bush, the first thing that strikes him is the oddness of the situation. Here is a bush that is burning and yet it is not consumed. One could argue that the spiritual life begins with a sense of oddness. Something occurs that is strange and inexplicable. A person who has never been "religious" suddenly begins to have spiritual leanings. This is odd. The person who "has it all," who has built an outwardly successful life with a good career, a great family, a fabulous house, and a "destination" vacation every year, begins to feel restless and dissatisfied. This is very odd. When someone says, "I have never been religious, but . . . ," the oddness is contained in the word "but."

Many people's spiritual lives begin with a sense of oddness.

Turning Aside

Moses stops and says, "I must turn aside and look at this great sight" (Exodus 3:3). After one has experienced a sense of oddness in one's life, then the next step is to "turn aside." This is difficult for Americans living in our hypercharged twenty-first century. Our society does not give us permission. Our busy lives do not seem to allow for it. We don't even stop for vacations. Americans typically eat at their desk, work during their vacations, and leave vacation days unclaimed. But turning aside and stopping is necessary not only for our spiritual lives. It is necessary for our sanity and emotional well-being.

About once a season, I put an excursion on my calendar. It is a day hiking trip to the Appalachian Trail a couple of hours north of our house. I gather my pack, put on my hiking shoes, grab a couple of energy bars, and I am off. Two hours later, I am alone in a hundred square miles of wilderness seventy miles west of New York City. Each time brings an adventure. It could be something as dramatic as seeing a mother bear and her two cubs cross the trail directly in front of me, or as quiet as watching a line of melting ice on a pond four miles up the trail. There is no phone, no computer, and no sound other than the sounds of the wind and the cry of the hawks. I always return from the Appalachian Trail with a renewed sense of who I am and how God is speaking to me at this moment of my life. Periodic turning aside and stopping is not a personal indulgence. It is a necessity.

Moses is struck by the oddness of a bush that is burning and yet not consumed, and he "turns aside" to see this great sight. And at this point God breaks through and initiates a conversation. A very strange conversation. God begins with an introduction: "I am the God of your father, the God of Abraham, the God of Isaac, and the God of Jacob" (Exodus 3:6). Now let's stop here for a moment. Moses doesn't know who this is? Moses is later identified as the only man who ever spoke to God face-to-face (Exodus 3:11). He is remembered as one who had a close and personal relationship with God. And yet this conversation has an odd, "Hello, Mr. Moses, I am Mr. God" quality to it. What gives? It is as though Moses is meeting God for the first time. We have the feeling that, up until now, God has not played a personal part in Moses's life. In this Moses is typical of many of us when we begin our spiritual journey, that we seem to be meeting God, or at least some spiritual reality, for the first time in our lives.

Also, like us, Moses is feeling some degree of trepidation when he first encounters a spiritual reality. We read that "Moses hid his face, for he was afraid to look at God" (Exodus 3:6). When we first begin to take the possibility of faith seriously, we too may have no small amount of trepidation. We may worry about commitment. What does God (or the church) expect of me in terms of time and energy? I have so much going on in my life right now, and now this? We may become aware of past behavior, or even current behavior, which may not be consistent with our newfound spiritual beliefs. Finally, many people carry memories of how they have been hurt by the church. A three-year-old in my previous church came home in tears from a Vacation Bible School run by a conservative denomination. It turned out that her teacher told the class that people who smoked were going to go to hell, and since she knew her father smoked, the prospects for her father did not look good. Like this three-year-old, many of us have things to overcome before we can be in a relationship with God or the church. This may help explain what happens next.

A New Mission

God tells Moses he has a job for him. "The cry of the Israelites has now come to me; I have also seen how the Egyptians oppress them. So come, I will send you to Pharaoh to bring my people, the Israelites, out of Egypt" (Exodus 3:9–10).

Upon hearing these words, does Moses stand to attention and say, "I'm on it, Lord. Leave it to me"? Not so much. Moses gives every excuse in the book. Who am I to undertake such an important mission? If people ask, who is sending me, what shall I say? What about my competence, Lord? I'm not very eloquent. The Lord counters every excuse Moses offers and orders him to start the mission.

I don't know if you have ever wondered what you would do if God spoke directly to you. If you have, you probably imagine yourself immediately jumping to the Lord's command. The story of Moses, and scripture in general, suggests something quite different is likely to happen. Your first reaction is more likely to be resistance. The prophet Isaiah, after his vision of the Lord in the temple, is unusual in that he immediately responds, "Here am I; send me" (Isaiah 6:8). The more typical human response is likely to be delay, resistance, and excuses.

I remember the day I applied to seminary. At the time, I was teaching school in Connecticut. For some time, I had been mulling over the decision. Finally, one gorgeous fall day walking on a country road near the school, I made my decision. I would bite the bullet.

I would go to seminary. I would apply for the next year. I looked at my calendar and set aside a day for completing the application. I looked forward to it with eager anticipation. "This is going to be the greatest day of my life," I thought. "I'm finally going to seminary. I'm doing what God is calling me to do. I'm beginning the journey."

The day came and it was the worst day of my life. Every doubt, every reservation, every sense of personal inadequacy came piling in upon me. What did I think I was doing? Did I even believe in God? What made me think I was called? What was a call anyway? How could I know for sure? The only way I succeeded in completing the application was literally by gutting it through. I forced myself to complete the form. But I still remember the pain of that day when all my doubts and reservations came piling on.

Moses has his encounter with God, which he struggles to understand and accept. But along with this encounter he gets something else. He gets a new mission in life. And it is not just *any* mission. It is a mission uniquely suited to his gifts, abilities, and previous life experiences. As with all of us when we sense a call, God is calling Moses to a task for which he is uniquely suited.

Moses has always had a passion for justice. He identifies with those who are being mistreated by others or abused by the system. He sees the Hebrew people as "his people." He stands up in defense of the Hebrew slave who was being beaten and, later, of the women at the well who were being chased away by the shepherds. The fact is, Moses speaks a "dual language." Raised as an Egyptian, he speaks the Egyptians' language and understands their customs and ways. At the same time, however, his heart speaks the Hebrews' language. He feels their suffering under their Egyptian taskmasters and empathizes with their desire for freedom. Even Moses's anger, which as we've seen can be volcanic and even lethal, can be turned to good when it is turned into righteous anger in service of the cause of justice. All of this makes Moses the perfect instrument of the Lord to free the Hebrew people from their slavery in Egypt.

But Moses also has something else. He has a "wound." Writer Henri Nouwen coined the phrase "wounded healer" to describe one who is wounded by life's circumstances and yet who finds in that very wound a means of healing for others.[22] Moses is such a person. His wound is the conflict he feels in his divided loyalty between the Hebrews of his birth and the Egyptians of his upbringing. This wound, which causes him such suffering as a young man, is finally resolved into a means of healing for his people, the Hebrews, whom he leads to freedom.

Moses's life has an important lesson for us. The very thing that has caused us the greatest grief can, if resolved, become a source of healing for others. How many people have struggled with alcoholism or substance abuse and later become gifted and effective substance abuse counselors, speaking to others with conviction out of their own experience? How many people have suffered difficult childhoods and go on to become counselors or educators helping troubled young people? In this way, our "problem" becomes the basis, not only of a life work, but a means of healing for others. When we get frustrated with someone, we sometimes derisively ask, "What is your *problem*?" This is a very good question if put to ourselves. We need to ask, "What is *my* problem?" If we can identity our "problem," if we can name the very thing that has caused us grief in our own life, and then resolve it, we ourselves may become, like Moses and other great spiritual heroes, a "wounded healer" for others.

Life Lessons

What does the story of Moses tell us about coming to faith?

Probably we have all had spiritual or religious experiences or times when we felt we were standing on "holy ground." These experiences may have occurred at any age and under a variety of circumstances. We may have been at church, or out in nature, or reacting to a dramatic change in our life.

Experiencing spiritual reality for the first time may have felt like being in the "far side of the wilderness." We felt "out there," far away from familiar landmarks in our life. Everything seemed strange, unfamiliar, and a little scary.

At such a time we felt compelled to "turn aside." We felt the need to stop and listen to God, or at least to our new perceptions. We felt the desire to get away and come to a new understanding of our self and our life.

This experience may have coincided with a strong sense of mission or calling. The nature of this mission may have revealed "our people"—those for whom we feel called to work or minister.

Our mission in life may be strongly related to an issue or burden we have been carrying. This issue has been a problem or "wound" we have struggled with throughout life. If we can resolve it for ourselves, we may become a "wounded healer" for others.

Reflect

1. When have you had profound spiritual or religious experiences in your life? Where were you and what were the circumstances?

2. How did you respond to the experience? Did you embrace it or where you unsettled by it? How did it change your life?

3. What would you identify as your problem or "wound"? What is the issue you have consistently struggled with throughout life? Have you resolved this problem or is resolving it still a work in progress?

4. Who are your "people"? Who would you like to serve with in a common mission? Who are the people struggling with the same issue you have struggled with whom you feel called to serve?

CHAPTER 6

Finding Meaning and Purpose

How can anyone be born after having grown old? Can one enter a second time into the mother's womb and be born?

—John 3:4

The year I retired, I made a "bucket list" of things I wanted to do. Some were modest, like going back to a restaurant my wife and I had enjoyed in the past. Others were bigger and more ambitious—like a long-anticipated trip to Iceland. There were finally thirty-eight items on the list.

I wish I could say that my reason for compiling the list was a sense of eager anticipation of retirement. Not so much. The real reason was absolute terror. I was petrified at the possibility of not having enough to do. I pictured in my mind the first few days and weeks of retirement: Monday morning, nine o'clock, ten o'clock, eleven o'clock; the next day, Tuesday, then Wednesday, then Thursday, and the rest of the week; then the next week, and the week after, and the week after that, stretching away into an infinity of time.

My mother had died at ninety-six. I was in my early sixties. I could easily anticipate thirty or more years in retirement. I could spend as long in retirement as I had working.

What was I going to do with all that time? It was around this time that I saw this sign on a man's T-shirt.

Eat
Sleep
Golf
Repeat

Being a golfer myself, I totally got the humor. But I also had to ask if golfing was enough for a *life*? Does playing golf every day give life a sense of meaning and purpose?

Around that time I overheard a conversation between two men in the local diner. One man said, "So Joe, how is retirement?"

The other replied, "Boring as hell."

The conversation reflected my worst fears about retirement, that I would not just be bored but would experience a sense of desperation at not having enough to do.

I thought back to the movie *About Schmidt* starring Jack Nicholson, which is a cautionary tale about the potential pitfalls of retirement.[23] Nicholson plays Warren Schmidt, a sixty-six-year-old recently retired insurance actuary. He and his wife are looking forward to a carefree cross-country motor trip in retirement, when she dies of a massive heart attack. Suddenly Schmidt has nothing to do and nowhere to go. His former colleagues have no interest in being contacted by him from time to time with "advice" about work. Schmidt's grown daughter has her own life and has little time for her father. Schmidt's life begins to spiral down. He wonders what he has accomplished in life and feels his life has made no difference.

The one bright spot in his life is his pen-pal relationship with a six-year-old foster child in Africa, named Ndugu. His letters to Ndugu function as a kind of ongoing journal of his struggles with retirement and with his life. In the last scene, Schmidt is moved to tears by a drawing the six-year-old Ndugu sends. This scene contains perhaps a germ of hope that Schmidt may be able to rebuild his life and move on.

But it has been a struggle.

The good news for all of us as we approach retirement is that we do not forfeit our need to be actively engaged just because we have retired. Humans are creative and productive by nature. The fact that we don't have a commitment to be in a certain place at a certain time, or that we receive a pension or a Social Security check instead of a pay stub, does not change our need to be creative and engaged.

Generativity versus Stagnation

Psychologist Eric Erikson has provided us a valuable map of the stages of adult life, from early adulthood to old age. He presents each stage as a tension between a negative and a positive outcome. Retirement, and the senior years in general, are a time of what he calls "Generativity vs. Stagnation." On one hand is the temptation to stop growing and living and to vegetate in front of the TV. We have all seen examples of this in our own lives. On the other hand, these years present us opportunities to be generative—to continue to invest time and energies in others and in creative pursuits.

This possibility can be enhanced during retirement, giving many the time and resources to be creative and engaged in ways that they had not been able to be before. Erikson asserts that a man or woman in the senior years "needs to be needed." Generativity, he concludes, "is primarily the concern in establishing and guiding the next generation."[24] This guiding of the next generation can be accomplished by mentoring a younger colleague, writing your memoirs, or even painting a beautiful picture to be passed on to others.

A story in scripture that dramatizes the challenges of the senior years is the story of Nicodemus, a member of the Jewish ruling council, the Sanhedrin, told in John 3. On one level it is the story of one man's search for spiritual truth. On another level, it is an account of every person's search for meaning and purpose, especially in the senior years.

We first meet Nicodemus when he comes to Jesus "by night." That choice of words is fascinating. Jesus is under suspicion by the religious authorities. Nicodemus is a high-placed member of the ruling council. He is a public figure, known and recognized. It would make sense that he would not want to be associated with Jesus, by this time a controversial religious figure.

Does Nicodemus come to Jesus under the cover of darkness so he will not be recognized? Or does he come to Jesus in a metaphorical "dark night of the soul," feeling lost and at a dead-end in his life? Certainly, this "dark night" can happen at any time in life, but it can also occur in the senior years, when many of life's familiar benchmarks seem to have disappeared and we may be searching for new directions.

Nicodemus comes "by night" and he and Jesus engage in a fascinating conversation. Clearly Nicodemus recognizes Jesus as a person of spiritual authority.

"We know that you are a teacher who has come from God," he tells Jesus, "for no one can do these signs that you do apart from the presence of God" (John 3:2).

Jesus goes on to speak of the necessity of being "born from above."

Nicodemus counters, "How can anyone be born after having grown old? Can one enter a second time into the mother's womb and be born?" (John 3:4).

Jesus picks up on Nicodemus's literalistic frame of mind, which is keeping him from understanding deeper spiritual truths.

"Are you a teacher of Israel, and yet you do not understand these things?" (John 3:10).

The conversation seems to end inconclusively. One is left wondering if this encounter between Jesus and Nicodemus went anywhere or will have any effect on the life of Nicodemus.

Being "Born Again"

The key to the encounter was the question Nicodemus asked Jesus early in the conversation: "How can anyone be born after having grown old? Can one enter a second time into the mother's womb?"

What Nicodemus seems to be asking is, how can one find a sense of meaning and purpose in the senior years? Can one reinvent oneself? Can one be "born again" into a new sense of purpose, even as an older person? Is the latter part of life something to look forward to, or is the best behind us? Is there a purpose to life in the senior years? And if there is a purpose, what is it and how does one discover it?

These are questions we struggle with as seniors. The truth is that previous habits of mind, habits that have served us well in the past, may make it difficult for us to find new paths in the senior years.

Nicodemus is a member of the Great Sanhedrin, the ruling council of seventy elders of the Jewish community who exercised a degree of authority under the Romans. The Great Sanhedrin in Jerusalem was the highest court in the land. During his career Nicodemus would have moved up from local courts, or sanhedra, in other parts of the country, to one of the two auxiliary sanhedra in Jerusalem, and finally to membership in Great Sanhedrin itself.

In being elevated to this position, Nicodemus had in effect moved from the appellate court to the Supreme Court. He had become a man of power and position, and thus he came to Jesus by night so his position would not be compromised. Nicodemus had earned his living practicing logic and close deductive reasoning. A career in the legal profession involves interpreting fine points of the law and a close reading of the nuances of language. This was the world that Nicodemus moved in. This was the mindset that had earned him high position and that he would have practiced during his years in the various courts.

The other side of a strength is often a corresponding weakness. Nicodemus was one well versed in logic, rationality, and the fine points of the law. As such, he would have been uncomfortable with any way of thinking that seemed to defy logic, rationality, and clear definition. Nothing in his previous way of thinking would have prepared him to understand or appreciate such qualities.

And then one night, during the conversation recorded in John's gospel, Jesus breaks into his well-ordered worldview, speaking of the need to be "born from above" and of the "wind" of God's presence that "blows where it chooses." As this conversation unfolds, you can feel Nicodemus's bewilderment. He asks Jesus, "How can these things be?" Nicodemus is far away from shore, way out in unfamiliar mental and emotional territory.

In this respect Nicodemus is like another man who lived twelve centuries after Christ. This man is Thomas Aquinas, a Dominican monk who lived in the thirteenth century, and whose thinking has been a bedrock of much of Christian theology for the past eight centuries.

Overcoming the Left Brain

Thomas Aquinas was one of the most brilliant people who ever lived. Considered by some to be one of the dozen greatest philosophers of the Western World, he was one of a select number of men and women awarded the title Doctor of the Church by the Roman Catholic Church in recognition of his immense erudition and theological teaching.

Thomas lived in the late Middle Ages, at a time when the wisdom of the Ancient World was being rediscovered and when the thinking of Aristotle was thought to be a major challenge to established Christian doctrine. Thomas took upon himself the task of reconciling Aristotle with Christian teaching and doctrine.

The result was the *Summa Theologica*, an immense intellectual achievement—five volumes in its original English translation—consisting of 3,125 separate articles covering aspects of Christian faith and doctrine. In writing this great work, Aquinas drew upon a variety of Christian, Muslim, Hebrew, and pagan sources—all the recognized knowledge of the time. The magnitude of his achievement is seen in the fact that his work became the benchmark for Christian theology even up to the present day. In temperament, Thomas was much like Nicodemus—heady, rational, and left-brained.

Three months before he died, however, something happened to Thomas that changed his life. Thomas was worshipping at a Dominican convent in Naples when he went into a trance. This experience, so uncharacteristic of his usual rational orientation toward life, was a precursor of things to come.

On December 6, 1273, while celebrating Mass, he experienced something that shook him to his core. Scholars debate exactly what happened. What seems clear is that Thomas had a profound mystical experience that made him question the lasting worth of all that he had written and may even have made him question the adequacy of logic and rationality to answer life's deepest questions. Shortly after this incident, when his scribe urged him to continue work on his *Summa*, which was near completion, Thomas replied, "I cannot after what has been revealed to me, because all my writing seems to me like so much straw."[25]

Thomas died three months later, shortly before his fiftieth birthday. One can only imagine what might have resulted had Thomas attempted to integrate his mystical experience into the *Summa*. Undoubtedly, what he had experienced was beyond words to describe. Like Nicodemus and many others, new truths broke into his well-ordered life, and they changed his life.

Let's return to the conversation between Jesus and Nicodemus. The story, as recounted in John 3, is an odd piece of writing. If one of my former high school sophomore students had handed this in as an assignment, I might have commented something like this:

I like your premise. Your idea of this mysterious conversation has a lot of dramatic appeal. Unfortunately, you don't do much with it. The theological talk seems to go on forever and doesn't reach any conclusion. Jesus and this Nicodemus character (where did you get *that* name?) seem to be talking past each other. Furthermore, the character of Nicodemus is undeveloped and not even very believable. Nobody could be that dense. The worst part is that your story has no resolution. Your account just peters out. We never know what happens to Nicodemus or whether he and Jesus reach some sort of understanding. You leave the reader hanging. This story needs a complete rewrite. You need a strong climax and a resolution. You need to tie all the elements together. Above all, you need to tell what happens to Nicodemus after his conversation with Jesus.

Fortunately, I was not the editor of scripture. In fact, the story *does* have a resolution, and a surprising one at that.

Stirrings of New Life

When we return to the story of Nicodemus in John 7, they are in Jerusalem. It is six months before Jesus's crucifixion. Jesus is teaching in the temple. The Sanhedrin is in session and plotting ways to get rid of this troublesome prophet from Galilee. In the middle of their debate, we hear a surprising voice. It is Nicodemus, who offers a legalistic defense of Jesus: "Our law does not judge people without first giving them a hearing . . . does it?" (John 7:51). Nicodemus is shouted down. "Surely you are not also from Galilee, are you? Search and you will see that no prophet is to arise from Galilee" (John 7:52).

Nicodemus's defense, half-hearted though it is, is surprising in that it came from this cautious man who came to Jesus "by night," afraid of being seen. But it illustrates an important quality of our life during the early stage of retirement and during the senior years in general. Often the first steps in retirement are provisional, lacking full commitment. We must find what works and what doesn't. Eventually we find our footing and move on with more confidence, but it often takes time.

An example is something that happened to me early in my retirement. A colleague had offered me a part-time position in a local church and my wife and I showed up early for the interview. She needed to pick up some materials at the arts and crafts store and we took advantage of the extra time to do so. I went along with her and soon found myself in the painting aisle of the store checking out art instruction books.

Art had been an important part of my life in high school and college. I had spent many enjoyable hours painting portraits and architectural scenes. After seminary, however, my art gradually dropped away. I didn't "give it up." I was just too busy. Life took over. Forty years went by and I had not picked up a paintbrush.

There in the painting aisle of the crafts store I felt my love of painting return. I picked up a couple of instruction books and checked them out with anticipation. I was going to get back to my art once again; I was mapping out in my mind the first of many paintings. It didn't happen immediately. Again, I let other things get in the way. But sometime later, when a church member offered to give me art lessons, I took the first step and committed myself to daily, or almost daily, painting. Today I have my own artwork framed on my walls. Forty years after giving up my art, I am again an artist. But, like many people early in retirement, I found that it took time, and some growing pains, to settle into a new routine and follow a new path.

Let's return to Nicodemus. As we remember from John 7, he offers his tentative defense of Jesus in the Sanhedrin. He risks his position and reputation to speak up for this controversial prophet from Galilee. But this small risk-taking, as surprising as it may seem coming from this cautious man, does not fully prepare us for his unexpected role after Jesus's death.

The Rest of the Story

Paul Harvey, a nationally syndicated newscaster, was known for the concluding segment of his program, which he called "The Rest of the Story." Harvey would revisit some well-known personality who had been in the news and give little-known details about their life. The "rest of the story" of Nicodemus is told in John 19, and it is a surprising one indeed.

Jesus has been crucified. Joseph of Arimathea, who is identified as a disciple of Jesus, asks Pilate if he might prepare the body of Jesus for burial in his own tomb. Pilate agrees and now comes the surprising part: "Nicodemus, who had at first come to Jesus by night, also came, bringing a mixture of myrrh and aloes, weighing about a hundred pounds. They took the body of Jesus and wrapped it with the spices in linen cloths, according to the burial custom of the Jews" (John 19:39–40). Nicodemus and Joseph of Arimathea place the body of Jesus in the tomb, the same tomb that is discovered to be empty by Jesus's disciples on Easter morning. Nicodemus, this cautious man who came to Jesus by night, is now willing to throw caution to the winds and risk being publicly identified with the burial of an executed criminal.

What happened to Nicodemus? What was the result of his encounter with Jesus which at first seemed so inconclusive?

If the story of Nicodemus were told in a modern novel, we would have pages of exposition describing what happened after Nicodemus first encountered Jesus. I can imagine the author describing Nicodemus walking the hills of Palestine after his conversation with Jesus, reflecting on his life and pondering Jesus's words about the wind of the Spirit that "blows where it chooses." I can imagine him thinking about what it would mean for him to be "born from above" and how that might transform his life.

Scripture doesn't give us any of this. We are left to imagine the effect of Jesus's conversation with Nicodemus. Scripture gives us only the Cliff Notes version. But what it gives us is enough. We know from what transpired afterward that the effect of Jesus's words on Nicodemus were profound, so profound that he was willing to engage with his friend Joseph to bury the body of this condemned criminal and to do this with seeming disregard for his own reputation and standing in the community.

Let's relate Nicodemus's story to our own experience in our senior years.

Releasing a Burden and Burying a Body

Old age for Nicodemus and his friend Joseph of Arimathea was a time when they carried a heavy burden and prepared to bury a body. When I read John's account of preparing the body of Jesus for burial, I am struck by the weight of the burden these men had to carry. They were carrying one hundred pounds of spices to prepare the body. They would have had to leave from somewhere inside the city, cross the city to the city gate, and go out the gate to the place where Joseph's tomb was located outside the city, all the time carrying the burden of a hundred pounds of spices. It must have been an exhausting burden. I can imagine their relief when it was over.

My wife and I have two dogs. We buy dog food in twenty-pound bags. A hundred pounds would be five bags of dog food. That's a lot of weight for two older men, even if they had servants to help. Either way, it would have been a challenge for whoever carried the load.

Old age, for Nicodemus and Joseph of Arimathea, was a time of releasing a burden and preparing a body for burial. But what if the body to be buried is our own? I'm not talking about making necessary funeral arrangements. I'm talking about another kind of body and the weight of another kind of burden.

Recently I attended a spiritual growth seminar where the instructor posed the question, "What is the burden you have carried for most of your life, and are you carrying it still?"[26] I thought immediately of "Busy Bee," which was the burden I had been carrying for most of my life, and the "body" I needed to bury to have more satisfying senior years.

Busy Bee was my tendency to be busy all the time. It was a quality I developed in my early adulthood and carried through even into my retirement. It was the tendency to be continually productive and engaged. Let me be honest: Busy Bee had been good for me. Busy Bee had helped me to have a productive and successful career in my chosen profession. Busy Bee had spurred me on to write four books, even during my busy parish ministry. Busy Bee had also helped me train and compete in marathon running. (What a perfect metaphor for being constantly "on the go.") Busy Bee had helped me get through some rough times in my life when I was able to escape into work instead of painful self-reflection.

But there was also a downside to Busy Bee. Busy Bee had stolen time from my family and friends. Busy Bee had robbed me of rest and relaxation. Busy Bee had cheated me of play. Busy Bee was, it was fair to say, a mixed bag. And, when I reflected more deeply, I realized that Busy Bee was a quality I shared with many others in our compulsively workaholic culture.

I decided to have a dialogue with Busy Bee. I tried to imagine what I would say. I wrote out this dialogue on paper, to help me clarify my thoughts. First, I thanked Busy Bee for all the times he had helped me. I thanked him for the achievements I might not have had without him. I thanked him for carrying me through some tough times. But then I told him that I no longer needed him. I told him that he had become a burden in my life. I thanked him for what he had done for me and sent him on his way.

With Busy Bee removed from my life, I was able to address other issues. I could rest. I could relax. I could give myself permission to not be productive all the time. I could give myself permission to play. During this time when I was divesting myself of Busy Bee, I had a series of golf dreams, and I acted on them. Busy Bee, I came to realize, was my equivalent of a hundred pounds of spices that I had been carrying around for far too long. It was good to be out from under the burden.

Combating Busy Bee is still a work in progress. Lifelong burdens do not disappear all at once. But whatever form they take, they can be recognized and addressed and acted on. And what better time to do that than in one's senior years, to free you up for the deeper satisfactions of these culminating chapters of your life?

Whatever satisfactions your senior years will bring, and they will be many, the senior years will also, inevitably, bring loss. Your health may decline. Loved ones may die. Pursuits that have given you a sense of satisfaction in the past may no longer be possible or be possible in the same way. How does one deal with the inevitable losses associated with growing old? Is there still life after loss? My wife and I learned the answer to this from a little white flower, the Matilija poppy.

The Lesson of the Matilija Poppy

My wife and I moved to Southern California soon after we were married. We took advantage of the weather one gorgeous day in early June and went the beach. In the late afternoon, we packed up the car and headed back to our house about twenty-five miles in from the coast. As we headed inland, we noticed a plume of smoke off in the distance. This was not unusual in Southern California during the dry season. Brush fires were common in the backcountry, and my wife and I were not alarmed. I joked to her, "That almost looks like it's in the direction of our house." We laughed and drove on.

About half an hour later we turned into our neighborhood. I had been tracking the plume of smoke during our drive and I said to my wife, this time not quite joking, "You know it really does look close to our house" As we headed up our street and pulled in front of our house, we discovered that enormous clouds of smoke were billowing up and cresting over the top of the hill behind our house.

We arrived to find our landlord already there and pulling down brush from around the house, a fire safety practice that Californians know all too well. I asked him what he thought was likely to happen. He muttered, "In California, if the earthquakes don't get you, the fires will"—not exactly the words of encouragement I was hoping to hear. The next hour was spent pulling down brush while my wife loaded up our valuables and our two dogs in the car. The fire continued its advance down the hill, finally crossing our property line. I felt the blast of wind generated by the fire and knew the fire would soon be upon us.

Then, amazingly, the wind changed direction. The fire, instead of burning down the hill, now burned around the hill, away from our house and neighborhood. Our house, and the whole neighborhood, was saved.

In the months to come, the hill behind our house was a picture of charred devastation. Even the coyotes, which previously had sung us to sleep at night, were gone, presumably to safer ground. And Southern California's weather patterns being what they were, with rain unlikely from June to December, the hill remained a picture of death and devastation.

And then, as winter passed and the spring rains began to fall, tiny white flowers appeared. Suddenly, the hill was awash with thousands of little points of light against the ashes. These white flowers were the first signs of life. Soon other vegetation appeared. But I was curious about these little white flowers that had asserted themselves so bravely. I asked our landlord. He told me they were a native California plant, the Matilija poppy. This poppy possesses an unusual quality. Over the years the seeds of this poppy fall to the earth and are hidden in the ground. Then, after some years, when a brush fire scorches the earth, the heat pops the seeds underground and they come to life. Only the heat of a brush fire is strong enough to burst the seeds. They appear as the first sign of new life in the aftermath of death and destruction, new life following what seems to be a catastrophe. Who knew?

In the years since, I have often used the Matilija poppy as an example of God's ability to bring life out of death. In the words of Jesus, "Unless a grain of wheat falls into the earth and dies, it remains just a single grain; but if it dies, it bears much fruit" (John 12–24). Joseph of Arimathea and Nicodemus thought they were preparing to bury a body. Instead, they were planting the seed of new life.

New life out of devastation. Life is constantly waiting to be born, often in the most surprising and unexpected ways. Our senior years are no exception.

Life Lessons

What does the story of Nicodemus tell us about the rewards and challenges of the senior years?

We may have mixed feelings as we approach retirement and our senior years. As much as we may look forward to retirement, dealing with it may feel like stumbling in the dark. If we experience a difficult adjustment, it may even feel like a "dark night of the soul."

One of the challenges of retirement is that often the very qualities that have worked to our advantage during our working years may prove to be detrimental. We may have to learn unfamiliar skills, like how to play and how not to focus on being "productive" all the time.

As we enter the senior years, we may become aware that we are carrying a burden of unfulfilled dreams or unrealistic personal expectations. One of our challenges is to give ourselves permission to lay down this burden and "bury the body" of whatever is impeding us from entering wholeheartedly into this new chapter.

If we are fortunate and self-directed, and rely on God for guidance, we will find new ways to be "generative" and to avoid the stagnation, aimlessness, and lack of purpose that can be a danger for some during the senior years.

The senior years are inevitably a time of loss. Loved ones will die. Personal health will change. Fulfilling paid employment may end. But God has a way of bringing new life even out of changed circumstances.

Reflect

1. What were your feelings about getting older and retiring? Were retirement and the senior years what you expected? What surprised you?

2. What burden have you been carrying for much of your life? What is that "body" you now need to bury to enter fully into your senior years? Have you succeeded in doing that, or is it still a work in progress?

3. Have you been "surprised by joy" in your senior years? What form has that taken? Are you currently involved with people and situations that bring you satisfaction and a sense of meaning and purpose? If not, what might be the first step?

4. What losses have you experienced in life and especially during your senior years? What new signs of life has God put in your path? How could you help this new life grow to fruition?

CHAPTER 7

Passing on Our Legacy

You see the trouble we are in, how Jerusalem lies in ruins.... Come, let us rebuild....
—Nehemiah 2:17

What is your legacy? What are the beliefs, values, and personal commitments you would like to pass on to the next generation?

Many years ago, I was on a plane beginning its descent. I had not flown for a while and I was white-knuckling it. As the plane began to descend, I was reflecting about something I had read recently—that the take-off and the landing are the most hazardous parts of a flight. At that moment, my eyes happened to rest on an advertisement on the back cover of the magazine in front of me. The caption, in bold letters, caught my eye:

What Do You Want To Be Remembered For
Before You Die?

That was not what I wanted to read just before we started down. Since then, however, I have often thought that it is a particularly good question.

How we will be remembered is not something we think about much during the first half of our life. We are too busy *living* our life to think of its long-term consequences. However, during the second half we do start thinking about it. I have a relative in his late seventies who jokes about being in the *third* half of life. That's when we really do start thinking about the legacy we might pass on to others.

A few years ago, I was teaching a summer adult education course at our church. I was within a few days of retiring and finishing a fulfilling ministry at the church, and I'm sure the thought of my own personal legacy was in the back of my mind. The topic for the evening was "Nature and Spirituality." Everything went fine until the end. The fifty people assembled seemed engrossed in the presentation and engaged by the topic. Then I began my wrap-up. It was a poem by Drew Dellinger entitled, "Hieroglyphic Stairway." I had read this poem many times in the past and it had always spoken deeply to my heart. This time, as I prepared to read, I could feel a wave of emotion rising inside me. I took a deep breath, told myself to get a grip, and began to read:

> it's 3:23 in the morning
> and I'm awake
> because my great great grandchildren
> won't let me sleep
> my great great grandchildren
> ask me in dreams
> what did you do while the planet was plundered?
> what did you do when the earth was unraveling?

surely you did something
when the seasons started failing?

as the mammals, reptiles, birds were all dying?

did you fill the streets with protest . . . ?

what did you do
once
you
knew?[27]

By the time I was finished, I was a wreck. Afterward I asked myself what had happened. The emotion that came upon me was so sudden, so unexpected. I knew I loved nature; I knew I loved being out in the woods. Our family joke was that when I visited our grandkids, the first thing they would do when I walked in was grab their coats to go outside. But this wave of emotion out of the blue? It was beyond anything I expected.

Then I realized the reason: the poem described the legacy that I wanted to leave to my kids and grandkids. Nature, and all it represented, was an important part of this legacy. And when you are reminded of your legacy, you weep.

All of us have seen the man who chokes up speaking of his "band of brothers" in the military, the woman who becomes emotional when she speaks of fighting for the rights of women and children around the world, grandparents who tear up when they speak of the kind of world they want to leave their grandchildren, impassioned individuals who stand up to fight for the environment or for gun safety. When people speak of such things, they are often speaking of more than a "cause," more than simply an *issue* they feel strongly about. They are speaking of something that touches on the legacy they want to pass on to others. And often, in the telling, they weep.

Subversive Grandparents

All of us leave a legacy, whether we realize it or not. Uncle Ray, who disrupts Thanksgiving dinner each year with his political diatribes, is leaving a legacy, although probably not one he intends. Most of us, however, want our legacy to be something positive. Our legacy is often something very specific, even while it is also connected to other values that we feel very strongly about. About a year after my lecture in the church, I wrote the following reflection on my Facebook page. I called it "Being Subversive Grandparents":

> We admit it. We're subversive grandparents. More than that, we intend to be subversive. We intend to pass on subversive values as our legacy to our grandchildren. For example:
>
> When society says it's all about "stuff" and accumulating as much of it as you can, we say it's all about life experiences and living one's own life to the fullest.
>
> When society says it's all about a safe job and a steady paycheck, we say it's about living your dream, wherever it takes you.
>
> When society says it's all about avoiding failure, we say it's about accepting setbacks as necessary steps on the road to achievement.
>
> When society says it's all about going along to get along, we say it's about maintaining your integrity, whatever the cost.
>
> When society says it's all about winning to make yourself look good, we say it's about winning by making everybody look good.
>
> When society says it's all about avoiding pain, we say it's about accepting pain and learning from it.
>
> When society says it's all about the Barcalounger and the flat screen TV, we say it's about getting out

in nature, even if your boots get muddy and your jeans get torn.

These are the subversive values we intend to teach our grandchildren. And we intend not only to teach them. We intend to *live* them. We intend to make a life lived according to these values so compelling that any other kind of life will seem like a poor substitute. And in this way, we intend to help our grandchildren join the other great subversives from other generations and from around the world who have helped change the world.

After I wrote this, I realized that I had written what, in the Jewish tradition, is called a "Living Will." This is a document articulating the values and life lessons that the deceased wishes to pass on to their descendants. It is a "legacy," not of money but of wisdom, for the generations to come.

In the last chapter, I cited Erik Erikson and the life stage he called "Generativity vs. Stagnation," in which older adults continue to be life-affirming and productive for the sake of the next generation. When we speak of legacy, we touch on the last stage that Erikson described, that of "Ego Integrity vs. Despair." According to Erikson, toward the end of a person's life, if they are fortunate and have lived well, they achieve what he called "Ego Integrity." It is, in his words, "the acceptance of one's one and only life cycle as something that had to be and that, by necessity, permitted of no substitutions."[28] The opposite, of course, is despair. When thinking about leaving a positive legacy, it is hard to imagine how a person could do this unless they had achieved some degree of "ego integrity."

An individual in scripture who wrestles with the issue of legacy, not only his own but that of his whole people, is Nehemiah, and his story is told in the book that bears his name.

Doing Well in Exile

It is the fifth century BCE. The place is Babylon, Israel's powerful neighbor to the east. More than a century before, Israel had experienced the greatest catastrophe in its history. Israel had been conquered by the Babylonian Empire, which seized Jerusalem, destroyed the city and the sacred temple of the Jewish people, and sent many of the population into exile in Babylon. This Babylonian Captivity, as it was called, broke the hearts of the Jewish people. The psalmist, remembering this period, wrote:

> By the rivers of Babylon—
> there we sat down and there we wept . . .
> How could we sing the Lord's song in a foreign land?
> (Psalm 137:1, 4)

Over time, however, many of the exiles adjusted to life in this "foreign land." One of them was Nehemiah, who had risen to the position of cupbearer to Artaxerxes I, the king of Persia. As the book of Nehemiah opens, Nehemiah has visitors from Jerusalem. One of his brothers and some other men from Judah bring news of the conditions in the capitol. "The survivors . . . who escaped captivity are in great trouble and shame; the wall of Jerusalem is broken down, and its gates have been destroyed by fire" (Nehemiah 1:3).

Nehemiah is devastated: "When I heard these words I sat down and wept, and mourned for days" (1:4). His emotional reaction is understandable, but it also seems extreme. The burning of the city gates and the destruction of the walls had recently occurred when he heard this news, and it is possible that he is hearing it for the first time. Perhaps conditions in the city were far worse than he had imagined. Or perhaps Nehemiah had never really come to terms emotionally, until this moment, with what the temple and Jerusalem meant to him personally and of course to his people.

The king, who seems empathetic and compassionate, realizes the depth of Nehemiah's sorrow. "Why is your face sad, since you are not sick?" he asks. "This can only be sadness of the heart" (Nehemiah 2:2).

Nehemiah confirms this. "Why should my face not be sad, when the city, the place of my ancestors' graves, lies waste, and its gates have been destroyed by fire?" (Nehemiah 2:3). The king asks Nehemiah what he can do for him. Nehemiah replies, "Send me to Judah, to the city of my ancestors' graves, so that I may rebuild it" (2:5). The king consents. He gives him letters of protection, and Nehemiah is on his way to rebuild the walls of Jerusalem, restore the temple, and reclaim his legacy and that of his people.

I have called this section of the chapter, "Doing Well in Exile." That is what Nehemiah has been doing during these years he has served as cupbearer to the king. The role of cupbearer was an important one. It brought one into the court, into the center of power. It brought one into the presence of the king, where presumably he would have been privy to state secrets and could even have influenced the king. The fact that Nehemiah was elevated to this role shows that he was both trusted by the king and presumably of an attractive manner and appearance, in that he would be seen by many of the wealthy and powerful in court. Nehemiah had indeed done well in exile. He had risen from being a stranger in the land of his nation's conqueror to become a counselor to the king himself.

In a similar fashion, many of us have done well in "exile." If our life has been fortunate, we may have married, had kids, bought a house in the suburbs, and achieved some small part of the American dream. We can look back on our life with some satisfaction.

But we also paid a price. Inevitably, there were parts of ourselves that the demands of work and family life did not allow expression. We lived, to some extent, "in exile" from parts our own self. Finally, when we reach retirement and our senior years, we have an opportunity to allow those parts to blossom. We have time to take those enrichment courses, to take up that long-delayed hobby, to travel. This is the great promise of the senior years, finally to come out of whatever "exile" we have been living in and to live out those parts of our self that were always clamoring for expression, those parts that perhaps relate more directly to the legacy we would like to leave for others.

This is the situation of Nehemiah when he has his life-changing conversation with the king. His years of "doing well in exile" are over and he is about to begin the journey that will establish a more long-lasting legacy for himself and for his nation.

When Nehemiah has this conversation with the king, most of the Jews who were sent into exile in Babylon had been gone from their Jewish homeland for well over a century. Imagine time-traveling back to America at the start of the twentieth century—before radio, before television, before the internet and modern mass communications, before cars or airplane travel, before most houses had central heating, when a majority of Americans still lived on the farm and in ways that had not changed for generations. This will give you a sense of how much life can change in over a century.

Similarly, much had also changed for the Jewish people since the exile—both for those who lived in Babylon as well as for those who had remained in Jerusalem. The Jews in exile, like Nehemiah, had adjusted to living in a foreign land by holding even more closely to their Jewish customs and traditions. The Jews who had remained in Jerusalem had forsaken many of their customs, neglected many of their beliefs, and lost much of their cultural identity. Thus, when Nehemiah arrived in Jerusalem, he found much changed and in need of restoration.

Nehemiah was not the first to return to Jerusalem from exile. The temple had been rebuilt during an earlier wave of Jewish resettlement. What was needed in Nehemiah's lifetime was to rebuild the protective city walls and to reestablish the people in their traditional Jewish laws, customs, and beliefs.

Under Nehemiah and the scribe Ezra who followed a generation later, the walls were completed, the temple rededicated, and the people returned to their traditional ways. Nehemiah and Ezra left as their legacy the survival and restoration of an ancient faith which, arguably, could have disappeared into history at the time of the exile. This is not only their legacy. It is also, in a sense, their "sacred dream"—of a Jerusalem whole and self-contained and at peace with itself.

Sometimes our legacy turns out to be different from what others would have expected. This is true of a notable political figure of the middle years of the twentieth century.

A Secret Legacy

Sometime around midnight on the night of September 17, 1961, a plane was shot out of the skies over Northern Rhodesia (now Zambia). In it were Dag Hammarskjöld, secretary-general of the United Nations and fifteen other UN staffers on a peace mission to the Congo. All were killed instantly.

Hammarskjöld had, throughout his lifetime, lived in the world of public affairs. An economist and diplomat and the second secretary-general of the United Nations, Hammarskjöld was called by then President John F. Kennedy "the greatest statesman of the twentieth century." Soon after his death, he was awarded the Nobel Peace Prize, one of only four people to be awarded the prize posthumously. The year following his death, a foundation was created in his native Sweden to carry on his peace-keeping work in the world.

However, perhaps Hammarskjöld's greatest legacy was a personal and private one only revealed after his death, and it was one that was surprising for a man of his political accomplishments. It was a spiritual journal discovered in his house by a UN staffer charged with going through his effects. Hammarskjöld had kept the journal from the age of twenty up until the month before his death. He called it a record of his "negotiations with myself—and with God." Of the six-hundred entries, one hundred related to God. In the journal Hammarskjöld described his philosophy of life and of service: "In our age the road to holiness necessarily passes through the world of action." Hammarskjöld's famous words, one of the last entries in the journal, are quoted to this day:

> I don't know Who or what—put the question, I don't know when it was put. I don't even remember answering. But at some moment I did answer *Yes* to Someone—or Something and from that hour I was certain that existence is meaningful and that, therefore, my life, in self-surrender, had a goal.[29]

The journal, published in English in 1964 under the title *Markings*, created a sensation. Here was a politician and statesman who also had a deep spiritual life. *Markings* was featured on the first page of the *New York Times Book Review*. Within less than a decade, it had gone through thirty printings. Poet W. D. Auden called the journal "an historical document of the first importance as an account . . . of the attempt by a professional man of action to unite in one life the *via activa* and the *via contemplativa*."[30]

Hammarskjöld's legacy is one we need today more than ever. Today, many view the spiritual life as praiseworthy but ineffectual. They admire the life of action, of worldly accomplishment, fame, and glory, but believe that such a life leaves no room for the life of the spirit. In Hammarskjöld we have one who combined both action and contemplation and who believed that each fed the other. Perhaps Hammarskjöld's greatest legacy is that he and others like him help point the way to reuniting our two "selves" and, in so doing, helping to heal our fractured world.

Like Hammarskjöld, our own personal legacy is not only the life we have lived outwardly in the world. It is also the more personal and private legacy we leave behind in the hearts of others. This truth was brought home to me during the seven years my wife and I lived next door to one of the oldest and most historic cemeteries in the country.

What's on the Back of Your Tombstone?

St. George's cemetery lies peacefully on a hill in southern Delaware, six miles from the bustling summer resort of Rehoboth Beach. The church on which it stands was founded during America's colonial days, in 1719, and recently celebrated its three-hundredth anniversary. St. George's earliest grave dates from 1732, more than a generation before the founding of our republic.

This cemetery was our next-door neighbor during the years my wife and I lived in Delaware. We joked that our immediate neighborhood was densely populated but very quiet. Twice a day I would walk our dogs through the cemetery. If I had time, I would read the inscriptions on the tombstones, containing the names and dates of the deceased, and often a citation of notable accomplishments. One had been a soldier in the Civil War. Another had served as a county judge. Still another had been a member of the U.S. Congress. These accomplishments and others were cited with pride. Clearly, they had given a sense of meaning and purpose to the lives of those buried beneath. Many had worked hard and sacrificed much for the achievements so proudly commemorated.

One gravestone, however, stood out from the rest. I discovered it one day by accident. On the front was the usual information, but on the back was something unusual. It was a love letter from the man's wife to her deceased husband, speaking fondly of their many years together and of the qualities that had endeared him to her and to others.

When I read this inscription, I contrasted this to the energy and effort most of us put into achieving the accomplishments that will be commemorated on the *front* of our tombstone. This is our "résumé in stone," so to speak. The things cited on the front of our tombstone are a record of how we invested our time and energy. They are what we wanted to be remembered for.

But what if these things are ultimately not that important? What if these proud accomplishments are soon forgotten? What if the things our descendants might put on the *back* of our tombstone are ultimately more important? What if the personal qualities that might be inscribed on the back of our tombstone are the very things that will live on in the hearts and minds of others and will in turn be passed on to our descendants yet unborn? And so I offer a question:

What do you want on the back of *your* tombstone?

The Butterfly Effect

At the end of the day, has our life made any difference? This is the question we sometimes ask ourselves and especially during our later years. Few would say that they had not lived their lives according to certain values. Many are commonly accepted values, such as belief in God, country, family, community, or the right to freedom and justice under the law. Or they may have been more specific causes or issues that they devoted a major part of their lives to, such as the health of the environment or the rights of women and children around the world. But did living out these values rise to the level of a legacy, that is, something passed on to the next generation and the generation after that, ultimately to affect the whole world?

Few of us have written a book that changed the hearts and minds of millions of people. Few have founded a national or worldwide organization devoted to furthering an important social cause. Few have been elected to high political office. Few have been "influencers" on a large scale. So have our lives really made a difference? Or have we been one of those who, in the words of scripture, "have perished as though they had never existed" (Sirach 44:9)?

Perhaps the answer is found in the work of an eminent scientist who lived in the middle of the twentieth century.

Edward Lorenz was a mathematician, meteorologist, and climate scientist. He was the founder of a branch of mathematics known as "chaos theory," the study of the behavior of dynamic systems. One day in 1961 in his lab at the Department of Meteorology at the Massachusetts Institute of Technology while doing an experiment, Lorenz did a miscalculation. This miscalculation would turn out to have profound effects.

Lorenz was a well-respected scientist. It was not like him to make mistakes. Like all scientists, he had been trained in careful observation and accurate data gathering. And his error was exceedingly small—less than two ten-thousandths of 1 percent of what he was observing, as measured on a one-hundred-point scale. Nevertheless, this error, as miniscule as it was, had profound implications.

What Lorenz was studying that day was weather patterns as determined by twelve variables, including wind speed, temperature, and air pressure. He was using one of the simple digital computers of the time—a Royal McBee LGP-30. He had previously entered his observational data with six-figure precision. That particular day he was checking his figures by reentering his data and running the program once more. To save time, instead of reentering his figures to the sixth decimal point, he rounded them off to the third, not believing it would make any significant difference in his projections. He started the computer and left the lab to get a cup of coffee.

When he came back an hour later, he couldn't believe what he saw. His data was now wildly askew, at variance with his previous results. Lorenz figured there was some problem with the computer. He suspected a weak vacuum tube. He checked the computer, and it was fine. Then he discovered the reason for the altered results. In rounding out the numbers to the third decimal point instead of the sixth, he had unintentionally set in motion significant changes in the data, hardly noticeable at first but, amplified over time, resulting in profoundly different results.

Lorentz published the results of his study in a scholarly publication under the title, "Deterministic Nonperiodic Flow."[31] His colleagues were intrigued by his findings and their implications, but they suggested a snazzier title. Subsequently Lorentz republished his findings under the title "Predictability: Does the Flap of a Butterfly's Wings in Brazil Set off a Tornado in Texas?" And thus was born the concept of the Butterfly Effect, which has had profound implications for a variety of fields, and which has even entered popular culture. (There was even a movie of the same title in 2004.)

The concept of the Butterfly Effect is basically simple. It is that seemingly inconsequential events can have profound effects in the future. The consequence of tiny events, rather than being lost and dissipated over time, as most of us assume, can in fact be amplified over time in ways that we could not even imagine. What that means for interpersonal relations is that even the little things we say and do, which seem so inconsequential at the time, can have enormous consequences in the future.

Spider on the Floor

Most of us are fortunate to have had one or two great teachers—individuals who opened our minds and expanded our horizons. Such a person for me was my English teacher in my freshman year at college.

When I think of him, I can still picture his dusty classroom in the basement of an old dormitory. I can picture some of my fellow students in that class. But what I remember most is the instructor himself—his comically irreverent take on life, his probing analysis of social events, and, above all, his evident care for the unruly eighteen-year-olds committed to his charge.

But here's what I *don't* remember. I don't remember a single thing he said. I assume that what he said was profound and wise and funny because that's who he was. I just don't remember any specific thing.

There is one exception. One day in class a spider appeared, crawling across the floor. Suddenly all eyes were on the spider. A red-haired boy lifted his foot to crush it. The instructor quietly said, "Don't kill that spider. That spider is more important than you are." Everybody laughed, including the red-haired boy who lowered his foot. And the spider survived, to traverse the floor another day.

I don't know what the instructor was thinking. I don't know if this was just a random remark or, just as likely, his way of showing respect for all living creatures, including even spiders. But I do know that I have remembered the instructor's remark to this day. And I wonder if that small event, along with other similar small events throughout my life, ultimately contributed to my own respect for life, which I have tried to pass on to my children and grandchildren. Perhaps the spider in my college English class is partially responsible for that nature lecture I gave at my last church so many years later.

In the final analysis, most people's legacy is not books written, offices held, or organizations founded. Our legacy is the little things—what we have said and done in our daily lives. Most likely we don't even remember what we may have said or done that made a difference to others. These may always remain a mystery to us. But for most of us most of the time, these little things may turn out to be the most important of all.

And our legacy lives on.

Life Lessons

Everyone leaves a legacy. Far more important than money, our legacy is the beliefs, values, and personal commitments we pass on to the next generation.

During the first half of life, most of us don't think about our legacy. We are too busy living our lives. We may be entirely unaware of what our legacy is or could be. But indications of what it might be and what we feel strongly about may reveal themselves unexpectedly as strong emotional reactions to a cause or a belief.

Our active work-a-day lives in the world, no matter how fulfilling or "successful," do not express all of who we are. To some extent we are "in exile" from parts of our true self. Retirement and our senior years in general provide an opportunity to return from exile and to express those parts of ourselves that were repressed or denied.

A sense of legacy, experienced during the last half of our life, is a sign of what Erikson called "ego integrity." It is a safeguard against ending our lives in despair.

Our legacy may be out in the open and available for all the world to see, or it may be private, known only to a few, in the form of memories, words, and acts of kindness remembered by those we leave behind.

The words that might be inscribed on the back of our tombstone are probably the most important legacy we leave behind. Far more than our outer accomplishments, this legacy will live on long after our death.

Reflect

1. What do you feel strongly about? What cause, mission, or commitment speaks to your heart or moves you to tears? How have you already responded to this? How could you do more?

2. What parts of yourself have lived "in exile" until now? What could you do right now to begin to express these?

3. What would you like written on the back of your tombstone? What changes do you need to make in your life to make these words ring true?

Notes

1 Gail Sheehy, *Passages: Predictable Crises of Adult Life* (New York: Dutton, 1974).

2 Joseph Campbell, *The Hero with a Thousand Faces*, 2nd ed. (Princeton, NJ: Princeton University Press, 1968), 35–36.

3 Aaron R. Kipnis, *Knights without Armor: A Guide to the Inner Lives of Men*, 3rd ed. (Santa Barbara, CA: Indigo Phoenix Books), 125–28.

4 Cited by Peter Stark in *The Last Empty Places* (New York: Ballantine Books, 2010), 176.

5 Ibid., 191.

6 John (Fire) Lame Deer and John Erdoes, *Lame Deer: Seeker of Visions* (New York: Simon & Schuster/Touchstone), 11, 16 (excerpts).

7 Malcolm Gladwell, *David and Goliath: Underdogs, Misfits, and the Art of Battling Giants* (New York: Little Brown, 2013).

8 Scholars tell us there are two different accounts of David's early life that have been conflated in the biblical narrative. I have chosen to follow the sequence of events as recounted in the first book of Samuel, chapters 16 to 18.

9 Joseph Campbell, *The Hero with a Thousand Faces*, 2nd ed. (Princeton, NJ: Princeton University Press, 1968).

10 Robert Moore and Douglas Gillette, *King, Warrior, Magician, Lover: Rediscovering the Archetypes of the Mature Masculine* (New York: HarperCollins, 1990).

11 C. G. Jung, *Modern Man in Search of a Soul* (New York: Harcourt Brace /Harvest, 1933), 109.

12 Ibid., 227.

13 C. G. Jung, *Memories, Dreams, Reflections* (London: Collins /Fontana, 1972), 217.

14 Glenn Kenny, "Racing to Save the Reef," *The New York Times*, July 9, 2017.

15 David J. Powell, *Playing Life's Second Half: A Man's Guide for Turning Success into Significance* (Oakland, CA: New Harbinger, 2003), 29.

16 John Grey, *Men Are from Mars, Women Are from Venus* (New York: HarperCollins, 1992).

17 Christopher Chamberlin Moore, *What I REALLY Want to Do . . . How to Discover the Right Job* (Saint Louis, MO: CBP Press-Chalice), 1989.

18 Hermann Hesse, *Steppenwolf* (New York: Holt, Rinehart/Bantam, 1963), 204.

19 For this medical information I am indebted to my clergy colleague on the staff of the Brandywine Collaborative Ministries in Wilmington, Delaware, the Rev. Dr. Marta Illueca, whose specialty is as a pediatric gastroenterologist.

20 Paul Hawker, *Soul Survivor: A Spiritual Quest through 40 Days and 40 Nights of Mountain Solitude* (Kelowna, British Columbia, Canada: Northstone, 1998), 16–17, 21.

21 *Close Encounters of the Third Kind*, directed by Steven Spielberg, starring Richard Dreyfus (Columbia Pictures, 1977).

22 Henri J. M. Nouwen, *The Wounded Healer: Ministry in Contemporary Society* (New York: Random House, 1979).

23 *About Schmidt*, written and directed by Alexander Payne, starring Jack Nicholson (New Line Cinema, 2002).

24 Erik H. Erikson, *Childhood and Society*, 2nd ed. (New York: W. W. Norton, 1950), 267.

25 Ruth Rejnis, *The Everything Saints Book* (Avon, MA: Adams Media, 2001), 111.

26 Dennis Slattery, "C. G. Jung's *The Red Book*" (presentation, Community for Integrative Learning of the Brandywine Pastoral Institute of Wilmington, DE, February 22–23, 2019).

27 Drew Dellinger, "Hieroglyphic Stairway," *love letter to the milky way: a book of poems* (Ashland, OR: White Cloud Press, 2011), 1. Used by permission.

28 Erikson, *Childhood and Society*, 268.

29 Dag Hammarskjöld, *Markings*, trans. Leif Sjoberg and W. H. Auden (New York: Knopf, 1973), 205.

30 W. H. Auden, "Foreward," *Dag Hammarskjöld: Markings*, trans. Lief Sjoberg and W. H. Auden (London: Faber and Faber, 1964), 23.

31 Edward N. Lorenz, "Deterministic Nonperiodic Flow," *Journal of the Atmospheric Sciences* 20, no. 2 (March 1963): 130–41.

CPSIA information can be obtained
at www.ICGtesting.com
Printed in the USA
JSHW051232170921
18762JS00006B/8